MW00477330

Angela Rock's

Advanced

Beach Volleyball Tactics

By Angela Rock

Foreword by Olympian Holly McPeak

Mericle Publishing, 2017

Publisher's Cataloging-in-Publication Data
provided by Five Rainbows Cataloging Services

Names: Rock, Angela.
Title: Angela Rock's advanced beach volleyball tactics / Angela Rock.
Other titles: Advanced beach volleyball tactics.
Description: San Diego : Mericle Publishing, 2017.
Identifiers: LCCN 2016916329 | ISBN 978-0-9979503-0-4 (pbk.) | 978-0-9979503-1-1 (ebook)
Subjects: LCSH: Beach volleyball. | Volleyball–Training. | Physical education and training. | BISAC:
    SPORTS & RECREATION / Volleyball. | SPORTS & RECREATION / Training.
Classification: LCC GV1015.5.B43 R63 2017 (print) | LCC GV1015.5.B43 (ebook) | DDC 796.325/82-
    -dc23.

To the women
who made beach volleyball what it is today.

Special thanks to Linda Chisholm, Kathy Gregory, Nina Matthies, Nancy Lengel, Roxanne Vargas, and all of the others who pioneered women's professional beach volleyball and over the years have given players the opportunities they now enjoy.

FOREWORD

The sport of beach volleyball has really come a long way in the last 25 years, and it is fun to read about the history of the sport from one of the best that ever played the game, Angela Rock. When I first started competing as a pro in 1991, Angela Rock, with her powerful jump serve, was the one everyone wanted to beat. I soon realized that if I ever wanted to win a professional beach volleyball title, I was going to have to beat the best, and that was Angela Rock and her partner.

By 1993, I was able to win my first AVP (Association of Volleyball Professionals) event on a super-hot day in Arizona with Angela Rock as my teammate. After my first pro victory, I knew that I loved it and had to figure out how I could consistently win at the highest level. The history of the sport from the WPVA (Women's Professional Volleyball Association) to the AVP to the Olympics has been interesting with many bumps in the road. The United States has had the highest level of beach volleyball along with Brazil, because of our strong domestic tours, but with the growth of the FIVB (Fédération Internationale de Volleyball) world tour, more and more countries have become proficient at a high level.

Angela discusses different philosophies, approaches, and parts of the game that only someone with her playing and coaching experience can do. Very few people worldwide have the credibility and experience to coach/play at the highest level like Angela does. Beach volleyball takes years to understand, but with this book, you get a crash course in everything, and the learning curve is accelerated!!!

Best of luck on your beach volleyball journey and enjoy the ride! Thank you, Angela, for your insight and teaching!

—Holly McPeak

CONTENTS

Acknowledgments   xi

Introduction   1

CHAPTER 1: PARTNERS—SURPRISINGLY AN
INDIVIDUAL SPORT!   7

     Developing partners
     Knowing your role
     Shopping around—the tryout

CHAPTER 2: TRAINING AND COACHES: "TRAIN UP"   17

     Finding a coach or trainer
     Practice partners
     Practicing alone
     Know your venue

CHAPTER 3: THE MATCH WARM-UP   23

     Warm-up outside the courts
     Letting them know what you are or aren't doing
     Practice all shots
     The coin toss

CHAPTER 4: SERVING TO SCORE   31

     Jump serve
     Short serve
     Line-to-line serve

Using the wind
Target serving
Selecting the target
Middle serving

CHAPTER 5: SERVE RECEIVE AND PASSING   39

Passing a tough jump serve
Switching sides
Passing the tape serve
Passing the short serve
Passing the deep serve

CHAPTER 6: SETTING SKILLS & RESPONSIBILITIES   49

Hand setting versus forearm setting
Blocker's transition setting
Calling the open area
Covering your hitter, especially on tight sets
Setting the end-line pass
Setting from a short serve
Height and location of the set
Back sets
Setting off the net
The "code"

CHAPTER 7: OFFENSIVE TACTICS   63

The head bob
Telegraphing
Covering
Shot options

High tool
Hitting from center
Hitting from all zones of the net
Setting off the net
Making the blocker cover more distance
Overthinking

CHAPTER 8: EFFECTIVE BLOCKING   75

Line blocking
Dive blocking
Delay blocking/shot blocking
Blocking the cut shot
Blocking in the wind
Pulling
Pulling short
Faking the pull

CHAPTER 9: DEFENSIVE VARIATIONS   89

The juke
The creep
Showing and taking away
Doubling up
The "I" defense
The game-opening shot or hit
Knowing your strengths
Reading and experience
No block teams
Psychology of the defender
The Rolodex

Baiting the hitter
Giving it up now for the timely dig
Taking away their favorite shot or hit—doubling up

CHAPTER 10: STRATEGIC OPTIONS 105

Playing the ball into the net
Hitting on two
The psychological edge
It's a great game

Glossary of Terms   115
About the Author   119

ACKNOWLEDGMENTS

I have been lucky in that I was able to play beach volleyball for fourteen years on various professional tours with some of the best players in history. My first big break was playing with Liz Masakayan, my Olympic indoor teammate and future FIVB Tour Champion, whom I credit with much of what I know today. Liz gave me the opportunity to learn the correct way to play from the very beginning, as she grew up playing beach volleyball on the beaches of Santa Monica, California. I was also fortunate to play with four other FIVB Tour champions—Karolyn Kirby, Jackie Silva, Nancy Reno and Holly McPeak—all partners who challenged me not only to continuously improve, but were role models in the sport and helped it reach its current level of popularity. Julie Thornton, Linda Hanley, Patty Dodd, and Karrie Poppinga were partners who reminded me to laugh at things and not to take it all too seriously.

Brooke Niles, Dianne DeNecochea, Barbra Fontana, Tammy Leibl, Daisy and Rosie Varbanova, and Lisa Rutledge-Fitzgerald are players I trained on a regular basis after I retired, and who inspired me to write this book. And lastly, Margarita Salazar for getting this book to my editor Linda Scott, and Megan Humpal for helping me believe I could get it completed.

~A.R.

Cammy Ciarelli, Holly McPeak, Angela Rock and Nancy Reno

INTRODUCTION

Women's beach volleyball has evolved into a competitive and highly technical sport, enjoying not only Olympic-level competition with athletes from around the world, but also as a championship sport in the NCAA (National Collegiate Athletic Association). As an athlete, I was able to play in two college final fours, five years on the USA Women's National Volleyball Team, fourteen years as a beach volleyball professional, and currently as an indoor and beach coach. Beach volleyball first became an exhibition Olympic sport in 1992 in Almeria, Spain. I am proud of the small part I played to help make beach volleyball an official Olympic sport. During that event, there was a bridge built from the hotel where Juan Antonio Samaranch was staying (president of the International Olympic Committee) to the actual volleyball courts. Every effort was made to impress him so he would lead the effort for beach volleyball to be included in future Olympic Games.

In Spain, I won a Silver Medal with partner Linda Chisholm and it was one of the best experiences of my professional career. We had been a part of a historical event and it was fantastic.

In 1996, beach volleyball became an official Olympic sport. Unfortunately, my partner and I did not have a great Olympic Trials and we did not make the US Team.

However, my friends Nancy Reno and Holly McPeak asked if I would coach them at the 1996 Atlanta Games. Coaches for beach volleyball at that time were not included as part of the official USA Volleyball Team staff, so the indoor teams added their "coaches" to the staff of the beach teams which did nothing to help the beach teams succeed. As the FIVB player representative, I was fortunate because I had a credential that allowed me access to the athletes and to Nancy and Holly—something no other team had. I was able to experience the Olympics from an entirely different perspective, as a coach. The frustration of having the indoor team staff not provide any real assistance to the beach teams and their ignorance about the difference in the two sports made me acutely aware of the need for specific information about beach volleyball. That was the moment this book was born. The separation of indoor and beach volleyball has been solidified now at the Olympic and NCAA level; however, there still are numerous NCAA programs that have beach coaches with little or no experience in sand volleyball. There is an assumption that because you understand and coach indoors you can coach on the beach, but they are completely different games. Due to the increased interest in the sport and the recognition of its unique strategy and techniques, the beach volleyball community is hungry for information about the advanced concepts of the sport. There are very few instructional resources for coaches transitioning from the indoor game to the beach, or for players who love sand volleyball and yearn for more in-depth information to grow to the next level. This book provides insight into the subtleties of beach volleyball at the higher competitive levels drawn from my thirty years of experience as both an indoor and beach player, as well as information I have gained from players I have trained. The purpose is to focus on the technical skills and nuances necessary to compete at the highest level of both men's and women's beach volleyball. Having worked with both men and women, I have found far more similarities than differences in their respective games. I use the pronoun she instead of he in this book as the majority of my experiences coaching and training were with women.

With that said, the attitude and the skills of a beach volleyball player are much different than that of an indoor player. An indoor player typically has a specific role—setter, hitter, libero. A beach player, on the other hand, must possess all of the volleyball skills. Of course, there may be specific roles that each player has on defense; however, on serve receive, a player must have all skills necessary to side-out consistently. More importantly, there is no substitution if a player is performing poorly; that player is just served more often, the pressure increases, and all weaknesses are exposed. This pressure is perhaps one of the reasons why the sport is so fun!

The transition from indoor to the beach can be difficult for even the best indoor players in the world. There have been several indoor Olympians and indoor All World players who have tried to play professional beach volleyball but fell short of the success that they had indoors. Successful transitions were made by those with the time and commitment to invest in the game. The most famous include Karch Kiraly, Elaine Youngs, Misty May, Liz Masakayan, Holly McPeak, and Kerri Walsh Jennings—all either played beach volleyball as a child or transitioned from indoor to beach quickly. I made that transition rapidly as well. I was an outside hitter who played all the way around and possessed the motivation and athletic ability to adapt to the beach game. The transition is not one that comes without a significant time investment into the training and techniques involved in beach volleyball. Many of the top stars on professional beach tours began as indoor stars, but some did not. For example, Jake Gibb and Sean Rosenthal never played volleyball at a four-year college and now both are Olympians—Sean is a two-time beach volleyball Olympian and Jake a three-time beach Olympian. It is not a prerequisite for beach players to be NCAA All-Americans, but it is imperative that they are hard workers, possess self-confidence, and are intrinsically motivated.

In reality, beach volleyball doubles is more of an individual sport than a team sport. The indoor team has six players who each play a specific role; on the beach, they must perform all aspects of the game. Like tennis doubles, partners can be chosen and replaced. The better you play as an individual, the more attractive you become as a doubles partner. In beach volleyball, you assess a player's talent and skills and pair that person with someone who possesses complementary skills and talent, hoping that the partnership is mutually beneficial. Because there are no substitutions in beach volleyball, one person can make or break the team's success. It is a team sport with an emphasis on individual performance. Poor performance will make for a short partnership, but good individual performance can propel players to a new level either with or without a current partner.

There are no secrets in sports—those who work hard and invest time in the sport make things happen. The harder you work, the luckier you get. In beach volleyball, there are advantages, of course, to being tall, jumping high, having fast reactions, as well as having great volleyball instincts. However, training and fitness are the foundations to beach volleyball success. In the big picture of all sports that are televised, I have always wondered why beach volleyball gets so little attention. Three times Kerri Walsh Jennings and Misty May-Treanor have won Olympic Gold Medals and yet the sport has struggled to grab a firm hold on the same professional level as tennis and golf. If it's exhausting for someone to simply walk in the sand, imagine the conditioning and mental toughness it takes to play several matches a day in the blazing sun, on the hot sand, with only two people on a court that is normally covered by six. If a player's skills are weak, fitness ironically does not come into play much because the match is over before she becomes fatigued.

I love the sport of beach volleyball. I hope that my insights give the reader an in-depth look into the game from the perspective that comes from my long professional playing and coaching career. In the course of this book, I will cover not only the obvious topics such as offense and defense but what I call the "chess match" of the game of beach volleyball.

©Megan Humpal

Tammy Liebl, Angela Rock, Dianne DeNecochea

1 PARTNERSHIPS
Surprisingly an Individual Sport!

Developing a player's special talent so she can have one or two outstanding skills is the biggest component to success. When I began playing beach volleyball, I was still on the US Women's National Indoor Volleyball Team, so my time on the beach was limited to weekends and late afternoons after indoor practice. I was a raw indoor player who could jump high and set well with my hands but had zero idea about the beach game. Because I had no beach experience, my first partners probably were very frustrated with me. Eventually, I caught the eye of some of the more seasoned players, and as I progressed and became more familiar with the game, my choice of partners expanded greatly. I spent numerous hours on the beach playing with anyone who would let me jump in. The best way to get a strong partner is to first improve your individual volleyball skills. Playing and gaining on-the-court experience is invaluable. Like any sport, nothing can replace game experience, even if that game experience is just at the local beach. Every playing opportunity provides repetition that can build player confidence; then it's just a matter of putting all of those experiences to work during competitions. It has been my experience as both a coach and a player, that players need skill execution on serve receive and need to be able to combine skill execution and brain execution on defense. The fun of beach volleyball is the strategy of how to make the court seem extremely small (with just two people) to the opponent when they are trying to score and how to find the open court on offense when hitting.

Beach volleyball is almost like an individual sport in that you need another person to help you. It may sound ridiculous but finding the right partner is accomplished by first getting as fit and as skilled as possible. Concentrate on your own development and then the right partner will come along.

When it comes to defense, are you or your partner skilled enough to be a primary defender? Can you or a player you coach increase speed and ball control? Can a tall player become a primary blocker or would split blocking (defending as a blocker and when serving, playing behind the block as a defender) be a better choice?

There is also the consideration of potential versus current skill level of play. Everyone can enjoy beach volleyball as there is potential in everyone, but not everyone can play at the NCAA level or professional level. As my former national team coach, Taras Liskevych, said to our young US National Team in 1985, "Potential means you're shitty now." I've always found this humorous, but not necessarily true as even the top athletes, performing at their best during a game, have the potential for more improvement and they aren't necessarily "shitty" now.

Beach volleyball is a very tough sport that requires patience, repetitions, fitness, and a high volleyball IQ. When I look at players and evaluate where their future may be, I always look first and foremost at their will to improve. Do they make excuses? Are they stubborn in their determination to improve? Do they have the internal motivation that can get them to the next level? Sand is like cross-country running; if you don't like to get tired or dirty, it's not the right game for you. As a coach, you have to look at players that are intrinsically motivated—without that, the possibility of success is not at all likely.

Who is a gem in the rough? I believe there are indoor players out there that may not be top indoor stars but could make a quick transition to beach volleyball. Lisa Rutledge-Fitzgerald, an indoor player from the University of Arizona, was one of those players who I trained. Lisa had one outstanding skill—blocking. It wasn't something I taught her but something that she brought to the beach from her indoor experience. Lisa understood about penetration, waiting on the block, moving her hands independently, ground position, and when to pull off the net. What Lisa also had was the motivation to improve the rest of her skills. I trained Lisa and she became a very good setter and an effective server. Her other skills were good but her blocking and setting were outstanding. Lisa eventually paired with Brooke Niles, current Florida State University beach volleyball coach, for several top AVP finishes. Although not an indoor All-American, she was a gem in the rough on the beach who had a very successful professional career.

What makes a beach partner a desirable choice for someone? The most sought-out partners are those who make their teammates play better, can better the ball (which means improve the next contact made on the court—typically making a great set from a poor pass or keeping a poor set in with a great hit), who don't make a ton of unforced errors, and who don't choke under pressure. For instance, the player that is a great setter would be a good choice for someone who needs a perfect set to be successful. Setting is a skill that a player can work on individually and can be improved with repetitions and dedication. A great hitter would be a solid choice for someone who struggles with her setting and needs a bigger window for their setting inconsistencies. A great defender is attractive to a big blocker. A big block is attractive to a defender. Those who can do it all—like Misty May-Treanor or April Ross—are the most desirable. They help those around them play better and can take care of their side of the court as well.

Knowing what you need from a partner from a non-skill point is also an important factor when pairing up teams. In an interview, 2008 Olympic Gold Medalist Phil Dalhausser said he was not a leader, and he liked that Todd Rogers provided that role for their team. Todd is a leader both on and off the court as well as a great defender; both skills were complementary to Phil, who is six feet eight inches tall. Phil is an exceptional athlete who at that time wanted to play without the burden of designing the defense or making the game plan for the opponent. He performs best when he can play in his zone and concentrate on what is happening at the moment. Recognizing that a strong leader was what he preferred, Todd was a perfect choice.

There are times when on paper someone may appear to be the best partner choice, but in reality they have an issue that is a deal breaker or they don't provide the intangible quality that brings out the best in the partnership. I was fortunate to work for a few months with 2012 Olympic Silver Medalists Jennifer Kessy and April Ross early in their partnership. These two women were extremely dedicated to their training and fitness. But what struck me the most about them is their absolute trust and chemistry as a team. They were perfect partners who brought out the best in each other. Jen and April could anticipate what each other needed and very little energy was wasted on negativity or problems outside of the court. I knew from the first time I saw them play that they were going to have a great partnership.

The long distance partnership—how far is too far? At the height of my career I lived in San Diego and I spent much of the time on the freeway driving to Los Angeles to train. It wasn't an option not to—there weren't any available partners for me in San Diego. But how far is too far? I trained Brooke Niles and Lisa Rutledge-Fitzgerald and at that time Brooke lived in Ventura and Lisa in San Diego. The drive was three and a half hours without traffic. This partnership had a lot of upsides—Brooke was a great defender and leader and Lisa was an outstanding blocker and setter. On paper, and for the first few months, this arrangement worked. Over time, however, it became extremely difficult for both players, even with success in the tournaments.

One of the last people I played with was Karrie Poppinga. Karrie lived in Hawaii and I lived in San Diego. This seems crazy but we both were experienced and worked well together to make this work. I would fly to Hawaii for a few days in the preseason and she would come to the mainland to train and play during the tour. We had good chemistry and we made it work even when we were thousands of miles apart. The point is that even in the best partnership situations, travel can affect performance and it is something to consider. Although if the chemistry is good enough and the upside to the partnership is worth it, distance can be a nonissue.

When is a partnership over? With professional or weekend tournaments, typically players can make their own choices about who they want to play with. The NCAA regulates college partnerships and limits changes; however, for those who have finished their eligibility or who play on various amateur or pro tours, when is it time to call it quits? I played with Karolyn Kirby in 1991 and we won twelve of fifteen events. The following year, we won five tournaments but I had knee surgery in the off-season and was not playing at my former level. After we had suffered a ninth in her hometown of Cape Cod, Massachusetts, Karolyn dumped me for a young player named Nancy Reno. We had won seventeen events together, but this significant loss was her tipping point. Much of it was due to timing. She was good enough to have her choice of any player on tour, and I was not what she wanted at that time in her career. The point is that you have to know when you've personally had enough. For each individual, there almost always comes that moment when you know—maybe the setting is driving you crazy or the choking is tiresome or the team has reached its potential and opponents have your number. Being loyal is important in many things, but in a losing partnership there are times when you must make a change. Playing beach volleyball is challenging enough without adding the strain and stress of a difficult partnership. If it's not fun, if you aren't improving, if you aren't winning, or the travel is too far, look for a solution that better meets your needs.

Developing partners

Training a young or inexperienced partner can raise the level of both players. Three-time Olympian and Bronze Medalist Holly McPeak, who has won seventy-two professional tournaments, used this strategy late in her playing career. Holly identified young, athletic, tall players who lacked beach experience and she trained them to become the partner she needed. Holly knew it would be helpful to have a big blocker to complement her game and instead of going after proven players on the tour, she would invest a significant amount of time training those who would become her protégés. It took guts to invest time and energy into players with the potential, yet very little experience, but it paid off. Holly was relentless in her training and dedication to her project players. She developed their skills and created the partners she needed in order to be successful. Holly raised the level of play of these young women, and they provided a big block for her to run around. Holly had a very good short-, middle-, and long-term plan that had a great return on investment.

Knowing your role

In partnerships, all roles are shared on serve receive; however, on defense there are specific roles that each individual plays. On rare occasions, the players may "split block" (when each player blocks while the other player is serving), but this is not that common. What is more common is a separation of duties. Players need to understand their role (blocker or defender) and take responsibility for performing it to the best of their ability. There are skills that both players should work on in every training session: passing, serving, hitting, and setting. However, a player that is a primary blocker should be training on her blocking and setting more than on her down defense. Conversely, a defender should not spend valuable sand time working on blocking and pulling, but more on defense.

As a coach, I believe that the down defender is the quarterback of the team. By watching and observing the opponents' offense, these individuals usually take charge when deciding the defensive strategy for the team. She can ask the blocker to change signals or discuss a particular serving target—usually a player they are more successful playing defense against. There is nothing wrong with having one person lead the team, but two strong personalities can also be a great combination if both can get along.

Knowing the role that each player focuses on is key to forming a strong team. Indoor and beach Olympian Elaine Youngs was one of the strongest leaders and players who has ever played beach volleyball. "EY" was tough physically and mentally and for most of her career she was a primary blocker. EY was not easy to play with because of her competitive nature, but anyone who played with her seemed to increase her level of play and won. Because of her competitive nature, she had high expectations of her partners and was tough on them to perform. This expectation was accepted because she was doing her part magnificently. EY was a winner and on the court she was a leader who made everyone she played with better. EY won fifty-two tournaments with six different partners and played in the Olympics three times: once on the indoor team in 1992, again in 2004 winning a Bronze medal with Holly McPeak , and also in 2008 with Nicole Branagh. She is a leader—and a winner. She understood her role and it worked well for her and her partners.

Shopping around—the tryout

Finding the right partner sometimes becomes a difficult process when it seems on paper that several potential partners offer what you need. Several times there have been players who I trained that had tryouts with partners they were considering. This is a very professional way to find out which player brings out the best in your game prior to making a long term commitment. Staging the tryouts with several partners during one session of training would probably be awkward, but if the players know what you are doing, no feelings are hurt and they will show up ready for the tryout.

Angela Rock, Lisa Rutledge-Fitzgerald, Brooke Niles

2 TRAINING & COACHES
"Train Up"

On-court training prepares you physically; off-court training makes you mentally tough. It seems like anyone who has played beach or indoor volleyball can become a beach volleyball coach and credentials are not required, just a tan and a good arm. Fortunately, USA Volleyball has created a Beach Coaching Accreditation Program to help instruct coaches on running a successful program, and the coaching has steadily improved over time. When looking for a coach, I think players and programs need to pay close attention to what will be most beneficial for the program and team. When a player is selecting a place to play during a beach volleyball college career, evaluating the coaching staff is very important. Beach coaches are a specialty and the game is significantly different than the indoor game.

Presently, due to costs and the desire to have a beach program, NCAA indoor coaches are stepping onto the beach and coaching. This is great for the growth of beach volleyball, but some coaches may not have the knowledge or experience about the specifics of this type of volleyball.

I have played for both male and female coaches and found that occasionally men perceive the women's game as slow, and will suggest that the women pull and play down defense more often than a female coach would recommend. A husband of a player I was coaching always insisted that his wife should be pulling off the net much more than I recommended. His wife was six feet four inches tall, and although defense was not her strength, her blocking was frighteningly good. I knew as a former player that if I was hitting against a strong blocker like her and she pulled, that I was going to unload and hit at her with all that I had. "Peg the puller" (hit at the retreating blocker) was and still is my philosophy. I think some men, with their additional height and strength, play down defense on a woman's net because it seems easy and they don't see the point of blocking at all. Of course, there are male coaches who have worked with women's teams and trained them successfully with the women always having a blocker. Three-time gold medalists Misty May-Treanor and Kerri Walsh had three different male coaches during their reign as the best in the world. Bronze medalists Holly McPeak and Elaine Young usually had a female coach. It depends what the player prefers, but there is no substitution for beach game experience.

Finding a coach or trainer

Selecting a coach is an important part of any player's development. Look at the coach's credentials—does the coach have experience on the beach? Is it primarily an indoor coach who is learning the game? If all you need is someone to initiate drills, then the amount of experience is not as important, but when writing a check or deciding which program to play for, make sure the coach has what you need.

Practice partners

When scheduling practice, should a team play up with the highest level of competition or play it safe and not let the competition see your training? This is the million-dollar question. If you play your competition, there is some risk that they may learn something about your team you don't want them to know but the exchange is equal. I mentioned earlier that I coached April Ross and Jen Kessy for a few months. Once when we were working together, Misty called Jen and asked if they would like to train together at Emerald Beach in Laguna Beach, California. Very deep sand, the best team in the world, of course we went! It was a great practice for all and Jen and April practiced up. If you play only with lower-skilled players or equally-skilled players, the challenge may not be enough to push you to improve. I have always believed that you cannot hide from your competition, but you should face it whenever possible. Train up. If that is not possible, get a coach that can push you even when the practice players cannot.

Practicing alone

When I began playing beach volleyball in 1987 I traveled to Santa Barbara to get some practice with legend Kathy Gregory. While I was waiting for our training session to begin, I noticed a player who was there alone, tossing balls and hitting shots. Lisa Strand-Ma'a, a top professional on the WPVA, was training alone and working on hitting all of the areas on the court. Lisa had a pile of volleyballs and kept hitting cut shots, line shots, hard-driven shots, deep middle, and so on. Lisa did this for over an hour, hitting then shagging and repeating from both the good and bad side of the court and from the left and the right sides. Lisa didn't have a training group that day but she took it upon herself to train on her own.

In the early 1990s, I would practice at Dana Point, a half-way point for me and my partner who was a Los Angeles resident. One morning prior to our training, I saw Adam Johnson, the AVP tour's best jump server at that time, at the beach serving hundreds of balls by himself, shagging them up and repeating. Adam was a great server and he invested time to make sure he stayed on top of the game. Both he and Lisa were dedicated to improving their play, and they didn't need a coach or others to work on the skills they wanted to improve on, only the dedication to get on the sand and work hard.

Know your venue

What type of sand is on the beach? Is the sand hard-packed? Is it rocky? Is the sand deep? Are the courts dug out? Are the courts east-west or north-south? Does the sand get really hot in the afternoon? Are the courts sloped? If they are artificial courts, is it a dirt/sand combination? Will you be on center court where there is no wind or outer courts where it's really windy? Getting a good look at the venue prior to the event and practicing there, if at all possible, can put those questions to rest so there are no surprises during the competition. Beaches in Southern California have some definite characteristics—Los Angeles beaches and Laguna Beach have extremely deep sand. Huntington Beach is also deep yet it is a coarse sand—also difficult to play in. San Diego, Del Mar, and Dana Point all have harder packed sand that is easier to move in for players. Man-made courts are usually hard-packed and favor the indoor players. Understanding the surface can help you mentally prepare for the type of match you are about to begin. Hard-packed sand allows hitters to jump higher and hit more effectively. Soft sand decreases players' jumps and they will shoot more than swing, especially when fatigued.

Practice up. Train with individuals who make you play your best. Train with individuals who will arrive on time and take it as seriously as you do. If you can't find a coach or can't afford one, there is much you can do alone at the beach or with a friend who can toss for you or help you shag balls. Invest in yourself. Take the time to be prepared physically and to know your competition venue. As a player, I would always walk the venue prior to the competitions. I would make it a point to walk or practice on center court if at all possible. I tried to do this the day before the competition but sometimes it was the morning of the event. I wanted to feel the sand depth, the wind, and visualize playing and winning on the actual court. Make sure there are no surprises and make sure you are as prepared as possible.

Dianne DeNecochea

3 THE MATCH WARM-UP

Any time you can get your opponents to think about what you are doing to them, as opposed to what they are going to do to you, an advantage has been created. The time players and coaches have prior to the match should be a time that not only prepares them physically for the match but mentally as well. I coached a team that would find a quiet place, and lay down and meditate prior to every match. No headphones, no talking, just ten minutes where they took the time to visualize the upcoming match and get psychologically prepared. When I played, I always needed to spend extra time on stretching and practicing my serving. Meditation was not part of my routine but ending on "one good jump serve" was what I needed to feel prepared for action.

Athletes also may develop some crazy "good luck" routines as well. For example, there was an AVP player who would, prior to his serve, toss the ball to one of the spectators who would throw it back to him. I loved it—the crowd was engaged and if he had a poor serve, he selected a new toss partner to see if that person gave him better luck. There are also superstitions surrounding attire. I had a weird one; if I lost in a particular bathing suit, that suit was now "unlucky." I did not wear it again until I played a first-round opponent who I knew I would beat and then it was deemed "lucky" again because I won in it. Some athletes have a particular stretching routine that gets them mentally ready or even favorite music. Find your routine and use it at the beginning of your match.

Warm-up outside the courts

In most situations there isn't enough time on the court to work out all the kinks or to practice every shot before a match. Therefore, it is important that you find an area where you can fully prepare yourself for the match. Drawing a court in the sand outside the playing area, finding an open court or a grassy area, or any open space, can all provide additional warm-up time. Finding a quiet place to prepare mentally with or without your partner is imperative for some individuals and not necessary for others. Establish a routine, stick to it when you can and modify when necessary; flexibility is important, especially when playing in a variety of events with different warm-up protocols or severe weather (i.e., wind).

Letting them know what you are or aren't doing

During a warm-up, both teams observe each other to see what shots they are working on, what side of the court they are serving from, and what is the state of mind of the opponents. For example, if you have a plan to serve a specific player you can make that very clear in your warm-up by serving every ball to the side of the court she plays, or of course, do the opposite. By serving every ball to one side of the court, players know they are going to see every ball on serve receive. Conversely, by avoiding serving to one half of the court, you may not be practicing what you will actually be doing, but you are giving erroneous information to the opponent; of course they need to be paying attention for any of this to matter.

Seeing the serving strategy of the opponent before the match begins may have an effect on one or both players' performance. Many players observe the opponent during the warm-up and they know they are going to be served every ball. I have also had players tell me in the pregame warm up that they know they are going to be served short or deep. My personal experience is the same. I would watch which side of the court they were serving and inevitably it was mine, so I knew I was getting every serve. This was a comfort at times and a bummer at others. Moreover, as a coach and player, I have watched the warm-up and decided which player the team I was coaching or playing should be served. Sometimes, this is based solely on how the player performs during the warm-up. I especially do this if I have never seen the team before. I can tell the weaker of the two players by how they hit, set, and pass in the warm-up period. This type of information (for instance, knowing the opponents' serving plan is to serve short) can help a person mentally prepare to be served short. It can also make opponents uneasy if they know they have a vulnerability to such a strategy. On the flip side of this warm-up, where you are putting the one partner on notice that they are getting served, the partner who believes that they will not be served will possibly not be as prepared to receive the serve. The question is, does any of this matter? I think that any time you can get your opponents to think about what you are doing to them, as opposed to what they are going to do to you, an advantage has been created.

The hitting during the warm-up can also provide information that opponents can either choose to use or not. For example, if you are hitting numerous quick sets, shoot sets, back sets, etc., then your opponents will quickly become aware of this and make a mental note to discuss the defensive strategy they will use to defend the various set heights. Of course, players need to warm up to be prepared to play, but also need to remember that they are always being observed. You can use this to your advantage.

Practice all shots

When warming up, you want to make sure you hit from all areas of the net, hit from both sides, and rehearse all shots and swings. It is also important that you receive from both sides of the court while your partner serves you. All of this is in addition to telegraphing your game plan (serving targets in particular) if you choose to use it as a part of your game strategy.

The coin toss

On a windy day or on a day when the sun is low in the sky, the coin toss can add a real advantage prior to the first whistle. Knowing what your team's strengths are helps in the decision-making process. If you win the toss, here are some recommendations.

Strong wind through the end lines: Take the side with the wind in your face.
Why? It's easier to pass when receiving a serve with the wind in your face as the ball flies truer and there is less movement. Conversely, when you serve into the wind, it's harder for your opponent to pass as the ball can drop suddenly.

Strong wind sideways through the court: Take the side that gives the partner who typically gets served the "good half" of the court.

No wind, but low-setting sun on the end line: Take the side with your back to the sun so you won't be blinded by the setting sun.

No wind, but you have a superior jump server: Take serve and start the match with the best server on your team.

No wind, but your serving isn't that strong: Take receive.

Most teams, without wind as a consideration, should choose to receive serve. Receiving serve is easier to earn a point than to earn a point serving. Both team knows their strengths and weaknesses and should plan accordingly. If your opponent won the toss and took the more favorable side (on a windy day, the wind in their face), have a plan for how you are going "to win" the side change down by only one point, or better yet, win the side change altogether. Side changes are done at multiples of seven or at five in a tie-break situation. A 4-3 or 3-2 side change would be great if your team began on the bad side. If teams do not set small goals, such as winning the side change, the point advantage over the course of the set will be too big to overcome with two equally-balanced teams. Imagining you are playing many short minigames to seven is a great way to keep tough matches close and the team mentally focused on each point.

Each time a match begins, players should have completed their mental and physical preparation as well as discussed their game plan for the upcoming set. The preparation can be somewhat flexible as long as it keeps most of its fundamentals. Routines reduce anxiety and a plan creates confidence—both of which are important factors in winning matches. Ask yourself: can you intimidate with the warm-up? Is there a particular plan you want your opponents to know you are going to implement? Have you practiced all of your shots? Which side is the good side? If you lose the toss, what is your contingency plan? If the wind is strong or the teams are competitive, have small scoring goals—win the side changes. The little things matter and the attention to detail in the warm-up is as important as the execution of the game plan. Use it to your advantage.

Angela Rock

4 SERVING TO SCORE

It's a strange phenomenon that players seem to direct serves at people instead at the open areas of the court. If you can't serve with a purpose, then you better have a great jump serve. When I played on the professional tours, I led the service ace category for numerous years. I had an extremely difficult jump serve, especially in windy conditions or on hard-packed surfaces. Once, in an event with partner Linda Hanley, I was having the best serving streak of my career. The player I was serving, Gayle Stammer, went into the Karate Kid "stork stance" after being aced several times (if you haven't seen the movie *The Karate Kid*, the main character switches to this stance after injuring his knee to prepare to defeat an attacker). Gayle decided that because she couldn't stop my serve she would just go into the stork stance and see if that would work or at a minimum make me laugh. It almost worked as I couldn't believe my eyes and I just about missed my next serve. After both teams had laughed our heads off at Gayle, we went back to business and we won the match handily.

Jump serve

Every player needs a jump serve. There are many reasons, but simply put it is more difficult to pass a jump serve than a standing serve. It doesn't matter if the serve is a jump float or a spin jump serve—either choice is better than a standing serve. As soon as the server steps to the line, it's an opportunity to score a quick point. When the conditions are right, serving a tough jump serve into the wind can be next to impossible to pass. Unfortunately, there are times when fatigue may be a factor with a primary blocker jump serving, and a down serve is necessary due to the additional effort of running to the net to block. Also, a player who is receiving every serve may wish to sparingly jump serve for energy conservation. I believe that a match may last longer if a team elects not to jump serve to save energy. Without a jump serve there probably won't be any instant points from an ace or a broken play caused by a tough serve. A longer, slower match is more fatiguing than the energy used to rip a jump serve and score quickly.

Remember that when a jump server elects to stand serve, the other team breathes a sigh of relief. The potential that a player has to earn a quick point from an effective jump serve, and the stress it causes for the passers, could create an advantage that could end the match sooner. Fitness cannot be banked; if you lose, you are finished and the energy you save isn't going to help you win. It just gives them an advantage because you are staying down on your serve.

When I train athletes, I make them jump serve and sprint to the net to block. I do not let athletes, especially when they are tired, elect to stand serve or have their partner take a turn at blocking. They hate it but the hard work must be done in practice. A tough jump serve is dependant on a great fitness level.

Short serve

Short serves are underused in my opinion because of the difficulty in executing or just from inexperience. A short serve requires the passer to do three things well. First, a passer must be able to get low enough to get under the serve and pass it back off the net because it's easier for the setter to set well from a pass off the net. Second, the player who has just passed has to be able to back up quickly for her approach. Finally, the short serve is effective is because when players don't do the above, they get under the ball when they hit. When hitters are under the ball, they lose the ability to see the defense and become easier to defend because of it. A good blocking strategy for a short serve is to block the hitter crosscourt. Most hitters lose the ability to hit line when they don't have a full approach and will swing crosscourt.

Line-to-line serve

A jump serve or standing serve to the sideline typically will force the player to hit a set near the antenna. Keeping a hitter wide has its advantages for the defense because a line-to-line serve will usually prevent a hitter from hitting a middle or back set. A wide sideline serve also will allow the blocker to close down the line more effectively by sealing to the antenna or give just a sliver of line if the hitter cannot hit line. A line-to-line serve for a blocker who is running up will also be the shortest distance to cover, and every step counts as they add up during a match.

Using the wind

I remember waking up on tournament morning, opening the curtains of the hotel room, and scanning the trees to see how windy it was outside to gauge the event weather. I hated seeing the trees blowing sideways, as I knew that the coin toss and side selection were going to play a part in the event outcome. To illustrate this point, once, when I played with Karolyn Kirby, we were seeded number one in an event and nearly lost to a thirty-second seed—a local Florida team. The team we played understood the wind better at their local beach and were used to playing in twenty-five mph winds. Players that understand how to best use the wind have a definite advantage over those players who are not paying attention. The coin toss, or however the choice for side and serve are determined, may be a more significant moment when strong winds are present. In windy conditions if the toss is won, side should be selected as it is easier to side out in the wind than score a point off a serve. To repeat, the "good side" is the side with the wind blowing in the faces of the players. Passing with the wind coming from the back of the court is very difficult, especially with a top spin jump serve that will drop once it hits the wind current. To reiterate what was said earlier, teams should strive to make their side switches as many points up as possible when they are on the good side. A score of 5-2, 6-1, or 7-0 gives a cushion for when they have to go to the bad side to side out. Conversely, when on the "bad side" with the wind at their backs, teams should strive to have the closest side switch possible—a 3-4 switch to keep the point gap to a minimum.

Target serving

Olympic Gold Medalists (2000) Kerri Pottharst and Natalie Cook developed a system where they gave each other serving targets as well as blocking assignments. This ingenious system not only directed their partner's serve but gave them a tactical advantage. Most teams just have a blocking assignment for each of the players and don't know which of them their partner will be serving. Giving a serving target to her partner gave the blocker an extra moment to plan and prepare to defend a hitter prior to the serve being made. They used the indoor service areas for reference, one through five and a closed fist for area six. One hand showed the target and the other hand gave the blocking assignment for the hitter who would be receiving the serve. If the server missed the serving target (therefore serving the wrong person) the blocking assignment would remain the same. For example, if the serving target was area one and the blocking assignment was blocking angle, but the server served area five (the left side player instead of the right side player), the blocker would still take that hitter angle. Kerri and Natalie won a gold medal at the 2000 Sydney Olympics, creating something innovative and unlike the typical routines of most beach teams. Target serving should be used with most advanced level teams who are looking for an added advantage.

Selecting the target

Every time players go back to serve, they have to ask themselves this question—who is their target and why? Are they serving someone because of their passing, their partner's setting, or who they think is easier to defend? Wind, of course, plays a part in that process, but when there is no wind, there should be a reason for who is getting served. There are only two people who can be served—or the open middle. Mindless serving is a waste of time unless the server can just unload with a jump serve and aiming doesn't matter. Teams should pick someone and serve her until she breaks or proves that she is steady. Make her play perfectly. If the opponent has an extremely tough serve, serve her every ball; it will make her think twice about jump serving as both mental and physical fatigue sets in. Make a player earn the privilege of not being served. If the partner can't set, force her to set every ball. Once you have established that one person is going to receive every ball at the end of the game, it's time for the "one off." The one off is the unexpected serve to the player who has not received a serve all set long. This person is in setting mode and not in a hitting rhythm. The pressure is on and they have not passed a ball the whole match. Test them. I've seen many a match when the big hitter who hasn't seen a ball all match shanks set point into the bleachers.

Middle serving

Serving from middle to sidelines, especially with a jump serve, is very hard to defend. Olympian Elaine

Youngs did this quite effectively and seemed to pull out an ace whenever her team needed one the most. Elaine did not telegraph her intended target with her toss; she simply hit different parts of the ball and jumped high enough to hit the perimeter or down the middle of the court. Because Elaine had the ability to hit all areas of the court, her middle serving was highly effective. Serving from the middle also means that the opponent has to decide whose middle pass it is. With no wind, it can be difficult to decide because both players are also worried about protecting their sidelines.

Serving is the only time you can hold the volleyball and score an instant point for your team. Take the time during training sessions to serve tough serves throughout the entire practice, not just at the beginning or end of the training session. A tough serve is completely up to the individual, and as I mentioned earlier with my examples of Lisa and Adam, it does not require a coach or a partner to train. Training sessions should emphasize serving from all the areas of the end line, into the wind, and with the wind at your back. Practice serving with delays and interruptions that simulate actual match delays such as time-outs and side switches, as these events often make players lose focus and miss their serves. As mentioned earlier, make practice a time for the conditioning aspect of serving and running up to block, especially with a primary blocker. The investment of time in serving always has a high rate of return in points.

Nicole Branagh

5 SERVE RECEIVE & PASSING

When I began playing beach volleyball in 1987, I was on the USA Women's National Volleyball Team and very focused on passing to the traditional zone seven area of the court for the setter. However, passing to zone seven doesn't work for a beach pass. During my first beach volleyball lesson, my teammate on the national team, Liz Masakayan, took me to the beach and explained the "L." The L is an imaginary line that extends from where the passer makes contact with the ball to a place where a letter L would end. The L is roughly five to eight feet forward and two to four feet toward the middle of the court. This area is in relationship to where you are served and shrinks as you move to pass a ball served to the center of the court to the letter "I" or straight forward. If you are passing a short serve, adjustments to keep the ball off the net are needed as well. Learning about the "L" changed my whole game. It gave me a mental picture as to where to pass and it was so simple to understand; it helped me transition better to the beach game.

Passing a tough jump serve

There are occasions when the opponent has an outstanding jump serve and siding out becomes almost impossible. Typically it is difficult to pass a tough serve because of the speed of the serve and the unpredictable path the serve may take—especially in the wind. There are a few passing strategies that can help diffuse the effectiveness of the jump serve, but they do involve some level of risk. A very good friend and volleyball coach, Dede Bodnar, was coaching Liz and me for the Olympic Trials in 1996. Dede gave me a strategy that I thought was crazy at the time, but I have since used her concept with teams I've coached. Making the jump server "think" about what you are doing as passers is the key. To do this, you have to make positional adjustments in your serve receive starting positions—where you stand to receive serve. When a jump server is teeing off with a serve, she is not so much aiming but hitting into the wind as hard as she can. This is a difficult situation because it's hard to get a read on the ball early enough to pass well. To neutralize the effectiveness of the serve, the server has to be taken out of their flow or rhythm. To attempt to control a jump server's serve location, tempt her to aim to open areas on your side of the court. A few examples:

- Shift both players to stack on the right side of the court.
- Shift both players to stack on the left side of the court.
- Both players shift to the center to make sidelines open.
- Both players shift to the sidelines to show the middle open.

The key for your team is to have a plan prior to making any of the serve receive adjustments. Will you remain in this position where you started, or will you shift back to normal serve receive once the server has jumped into the air to serve? That is the control—will you stay or will you go? Now you are making the server think about where to serve . . . the thought may be "why are the passers in such an odd place, and will they remain there or shift when I serve?" All of these questions get in the way of the server's flow and often give you a small psychological edge. There are many combinations of this strategy, but the point is to get some control back. You cannot control the pace or tempo of the serve, but you may be able to direct the location of the serve or better yet, make them miss.

Switching sides

Typically, one player will be targeted for the serve. The target may be the smaller player, the player with less ball control, the shooter, the big hitter, or the player on the bad side of the court. Serving the big hitter may be used to force a weaker setter to set or it may be that the big hitter is a weaker passer. Whatever the case, being the target of every serve becomes tiring, and the opponent can get into a groove playing defense time and time again against the same hitter from the same side.

If one player is having difficulty siding out due to the wind, one option is to put the strong passer/player on the bad half if the wind is blowing through the court from sideline to sideline. For example, when Olympic Bronze

Medalist Elaine Youngs was playing in windy conditions with injured partner Nicole Branagh, Elaine would put Nicole on the good side and she would play the bad side. What this meant was on one side she would play left and then switch straight under the net to play the right on the other side of the court—something that is never done on the professional level. Elaine always took the bad half of the court. She would tempt the opponent to serve the "bad half" of the court, but the bad side would have her receiving and she was the healthy player. As an opponent, do you serve Nicole on the good side of the court or try to serve into the wind and serve Elaine, the more experienced player? They used this strategy at a time when Nicole was injured and it served them well. When Nicole was healthy again, they played their assigned sides.

A funny story about a variation of this plan was when I was coaching Dianne DeNecochea and Barbra Fontana in an AVP tournament in Glendale, Arizona. The tournament was on a very hard-packed dirt/sand surface that was easy to move quickly on. Dianne and Barb were playing Elaine and Nicole, and Nicole had injured her ankle again but she continued to play. Of course Di and Barb were going to serve Nicole every ball, right? Dianne, at six feet four inches, had a very tough jump serve but windy conditions made it difficult to serve the injured Nicole, who was playing the good side of the court. Dianne decided to stay down and float serve Nicole to make sure she could get her the ball. When Dianne went back to serve, Elaine and Nicole would stand in the center of the court in a line, and would wait to see which way Dianne was serving. Then Elaine would scramble to the half that Dianne served to take every pass. Seeing a team in the "I" formation was almost laughable and it took guts to try it. The solution to this was for Dianne to jump serve.

When Dianne would hold the ball for her jump serve toss, the two would split apart and Elaine would take the bad windy side so Dianne would have trouble serving Nicole. For about a minute, Dianne would hold the ball to float, they would go into the "I" formation, then she would change her hand to toss for a jump serve, then they would split apart—back and forth the server would change and so would Elaine and Nicole. I've never to this day seen anything like it! Finally, the referee got irritated and told the teams to "knock it off" and that was the end of it. To this day, I admire their plan and the problem solving they used to stay in the tournament.

Sometimes the player who is not performing well and consequently is receiving all the serves, just needs something to change. Since I was served all the time, one effective option I used on many occasions was to switch sides with my partner. It doesn't sound like much, but sometimes it just provides a little breathing room and the defense has to deal with you attacking from a different area of the net as well. There is no pride lost when switching sides. This is especially true when the partner cannot or will not help on two, and the targeted player feels like there are no open shots or hits, and the opponent has their number.

Passing the tape serve

On the rare occasion when the serve hits the top of the tape, it's almost impossible for the passer to touch the ball, and this typically results in a service ace. One option is to have the setter, who has released forward to set, pass any tape-served ball. The setter is moving forward, watching the ball, and is probably in a better position to react to a tape serve that will drop short off the net. Obviously, if the passer can reach the tape serve, it would be a stronger offensive strategy to take the first contact but not at the price of being aced.

Passing the short serve

Serving short, especially to a player who is unfit, not very agile, doing all the blocking, or to a team whose setter has trouble setting a tight pass, can be a very effective strategy. Generally, on serve receive, the pass not only needs to be high enough to give the hitter time to back off the net far enough to make an approach, but far enough off the net so the setter can square up to the setting target for a more accurate set. When the ball is served short, one common mistake on serve receive is to pass the ball tight to the net, which makes it difficult for the setter to set the ball accurately. For the serving team, a short serve can be an effective tool to force a poor set or a weak attack.

Another reason to use the short serve is to tire out your opponent. It is physically taxing to pass a short serve, back up, and take a full approach to attack the ball. This is especially the case if the player who is receiving the short serves is also the primary blocker for the team. The cumulative effect of the fatigue may pay off in the second or third set.

The short serve, despite its attractive advantages, also has its built-in risks. One major problem with the short serve, especially if it is a quick short serve, is that it opens up the "on-two" attack. From the perspective of the receiving team, a short serve opens up the very tempting opportunity for the setter to attack on-two, especially if the pass is tight to the net. In this scenario, the non serving partner must be ready to help either block if they are at the net or dig if they are the down defender and their partner is running up to block or dig.

The server, who has served short and is a primary blocker, can actually be spiked at by the opponent's setter when running up to block—which is quite unnerving when not prepared to defend oneself. For these reasons, the decision to serve short must include the consideration of whether your team can effectively block an "on two" attack. If the opponent receiving team does not have a player who can attack on two, then it's a lot simpler to make this strategy work from a defensive point of view.

Passing the deep serve

Just as serving short is tiring for the passer, so is passing from deep in the court because of the effort it takes to approach and hit. A reminder to the passer is to try not to push the pass all the way to the net on the first contact after a deep serve, but rather pass ten feet off and progressively move the offense forward in increments. A soft swing of the arms to lift and guide the pass is necessary to get the ball to the intended area of the court.

Serving a combination of short and deep serves can be very effective as the hitter has to continually adjust and may have difficulty finding her rhythm. Any serve away from players that makes them move is more effective than serving right at them. Drills for serving should consist of serving the perimeter, short, deep, middle, or anywhere the passers would NOT be standing. Too often the repetitions that players get are from training drills that require reps to teammates—which is just poor serving practice.

The pass sets the rhythm for the entire rally. A consistent pass, that enables your partner to easily set you, makes the entire difference in the scoring opportunity. When I worked with Olympian Karch Kiraly during a camp, he discussed "tilt to target" when referencing how to direct a serve to your intended target. If a ball was served to your sideline, you would tilt your platform to angle the rebound of the ball to the inside of the court. He believed, and so do I, that it is impossible to actually face where you are trying to pass; rather rather dip your shoulders to keep your platform intact and angle the ball to where you want it to go. For short serves, a flat, horizontal platform is best to pull the ball back from the net. For deep serves, a slight swinging platform to bring a deep serve halfway to the net is recommended. For a hard jump serve, a firm "tilt to target" passing platform with soft absorbing legs is the base concept for successful target passing. Remember, when you are struggling, there are solutions such as side switching and shifting serve-reception starting positions that may help you side out more easily.

Karrie Poppinga

©*John Bartelt*

6 SETTING SKILLS & RESPONSIBILITIES

I came directly from the USA Women's National Volleyball Team to the beach, and I assumed that it would be much better to hand set than bump set. As an indoor player, it would just be unacceptable to not use your hands when setting and I could not understand why the beach players so rarely hand set. I quickly learned that the rules for beach volleyball are more stringent in regards to double contact, or "doubling" the ball, and any spin on the ball is prohibited.

Obviously wind conditions are a nonissue indoors; however, on the beach the wind can affect the quality of sets and whether or not teams can hand set as well. I was determined from the beginning to use my hands and developed a soft, beach setting style. Unfortunately, I had to learn the hard way (getting called for throws) that the set needed to be virtually perfect to not be called a double. I did not give up but adjusted to the rules and made hand setting my standard. I know as a beach player that I always preferred to have a partner who hand set. I also realized that hand setting made me an attractive partner. I was an excellent setter, and I know that the numerous options and the flexibility hand setting gives to a team's offense is incredible. Yes, bump setting is required in emergencies such as extremely windy conditions or on tight or deep off passes, but hand setting is just more accurate. Learn to hand set; it is a huge advantage.

Setting on the beach is different than indoors in another major way: on the beach, the person being set asks for the location and height of their sets, while indoors, the setter makes the decisions about set location and height. On the beach, setting is the skill that separates good teams from great teams because it has a huge effect on hitting efficiency. Communication about the set the hitter wants is a difficult change for indoor hitters transitioning to the beach game but a necessary one. A hitter can't get the set they want without specifically asking for it.

Training to set on the beach requires a whole new mindset. An indoor volleyball setter's job is to get her hitters either a single block or, better yet, no blocker at all. However, on the beach, the setter is giving her only hitter the set she wants. Whether the hitter wants the set high, low, inside, outside, tight, or off, doesn't matter. The setter on the beach does whatever makes their partner, the hitter, happy and able to side out. The indoor player delivers the set the coach wants, and the hitter must hit the set at the tempo and location prescribed by the team's offensive plan.

The beach setter is the exact opposite. She must listen to her partner and try to provide what she needs, no matter the quality of the pass received. The setter is the fixer of bad passes—always bettering the ball and putting up a set that is hittable. There is no need to "trick" the opponent's blocker since there is only one hitter on the court, unless the setter attacks on two, the person passing the ball will be set. Getting a partner to ask for a certain set is often the biggest obstacle, along with the setter being able to deliver the set to the desired area.

There are two things players can do to give themselves the best opportunity for a good set. First, setters must release to set immediately once they have determined they will not pass. "Releasing" means abandoning the role of a passer and moving toward a partner on a diagonal path to the net to intercept the pass. The setter is trying to give a target to the passer that will encourage a forward, slightly inside pass (remember the "L"). The goal of setters is to face their hips and square their shoulders toward the direction they intend to set the ball, while they turn their head to watch the pass.

One of the biggest mistakes setters make during serve receive, is instead of just turning their head to spot the passer, they improperly turn their whole body towards the passer. As a result, setters swing their arms to try to push the set across their body up to the net. Not only is this technique inaccurate, it is also difficult for the hitter to read where the set may end up. I teach setters to point their hips to the antenna (or the area of the net the set is intended), and they can turn their head to see the flight of the ball off their partner's arms and keep hips to the antenna. If the ball happens to be an errant pass, this of course is impossible and emergency pursuit efforts are necessary. On a well passed ball (forward and slightly to center unless passing from center) with the setter coming in from the right side, she should set with her right foot forward. Likewise the setter, when coming from the left, should set with her left foot forward. Why? Having the foot forward nearest to the net helps setters not to overset (because their stance is open to the court instead of open to the net) and allows them a well-balanced posture to follow through to target. If it is an off-target pass this may be impossible, so following through to target is the only alternative. Exaggerating the "thumbs to target" when bump setting an off pass helps the hitter track where the set will end up.

Hand setting versus forearm setting

The location and accuracy of the set are always more important than the technique used to deliver the set. That being said, hand setting is easier for the hitter to read and usually more accurate. However, due to the tight ball-handling rules, bump setting is still the more common beach volleyball setting technique. No bump set can compare to the ease of hitting a good hand set and players can develop the hands necessary for sand volleyball if they invest the time. A good friend of mine, Olympian Nancy Reno, was a middle blocker from Stanford University who, as she would describe, had cooking utensils for hands. One winter, she decided she was going to become a hand setter. Reno spent countless hours on the beach working on her hand setting and it changed her game dramatically. A big blocker like Reno who could also deliver a hand set was a very popular partner after her investment to improve her setting. As I have said before, setting is the skill that separates good teams from great teams. Having the ability to always improve the second contact is invaluable as all hitters are more effective when they receive a "perfect" set. Good setters are popular partners! Hand setting is a skill that can be practiced over the winter months or individually—repetitions and the commitment to use your hands can change the quality of partners you obtain.

Blocker's transition setting

Anytime there is a dig, a point scoring opportunity is available. The blocker now has to transition (go from defense to offense). This assumption is based on a team that is playing with a primary blocker and a primary defender. The blocker, at the time of the dig, has to land, turn, and pursue the ball to give her partner a set they can get a kill with and score a point. Because blockers have their back to the defender they begin the process of setting from an awkward position, and delivering a hittable set is a very difficult skill to do well. Earning a point from a dig is so much harder than siding out, but it is often what separates successful teams from average teams. This skill requires hours of transition setting repetitions from both line and angle digs. Once blockers have set the ball, they have completed the first part of their job. The second is to call the open shot, and third, cover their hitter. Always these three steps in that order—no exceptions!

Calling the open area

The primary responsibility of the setter is to call the open area of the court and to cover the hitter. After setting the ball, the setter should look at the opponent's side of the court and call the "shot" location. By calling the shot, you are telling your partner where the open area of the court is (where the defender is not positioned to dig). The defender is located in the half of the court that the blocker is permitting the hitter to swing towards. For example, if the blocker is blocking line, the call is the shot, an off speed hit that travels "line" over the block and deep. If the hitter does not want to shoot the ball (hit a shot) over the block, she knows by her partner calling "line" that the swing is hard angle. Thus, the call is to the open area of the court that the defender will have to pursue the ball instead of where she is standing to dig. The attacker, depending on her skill level, can elect to listen to the call or swing around the block, which is at the back-court defender.

When a blocker is "blocking line," a crosscourt hit is the first responsibility of the defender. If the hitter chooses to swing away and challenge the down defender, which is the natural instinct of an indoor player, she may find herself at a disadvantage. The natural instinct of indoor players to avoid the block actually makes them easier to defend in the early years of their beach career. Because they usually won't "hit shots," the defender doesn't have to worry about pursuing, just making the dig. The court is too large to be protected by one block and one defender, so there is always something open. Listening to the setter's call is a huge part of the team's ability to side out or score. I think that an accurate call is important in building team trust. As a player, I would always prefer a correct late call (if the defender is moving around and not still) to a call that was always incorrect. A player owes a call to her partner and then an apology if she happens to be wrong. However, if a hitter can acquire the ability to look at the defense behind the block prior to hitting, she can take care of her own choices and won't have to rely on a call.

If the setter sets her partner poorly and the blocker pulls off the net, the first information the setter should give a partner is the "no one" call. If the setter calls "no one" first, then the hitter knows that the "shot" must be well placed, or she can swing away on an open net without concern about a blocker. Remember, calling a shot implies there is a blocker up. A partner can also add more when calling the "no one" call. Where is the weaker defender located? What is the biggest open area on the court? Did the down defender ever come out of her base or is she still in the center of the court and the cut is open? Is the pulling blocker a good target to hit? A few good examples would be, "No one, line hard!" or "No one, cut" or "No one middle." The more specific you are the more success the hitter has with a two down defense.

Covering your hitter, especially on tight sets

There are three responsibilities for the setter: set a perfect ball, call the correct shot, and cover the hitter. Numbers two and three seem to be the most overlooked responsibilities. If you are not a great setter, then you better make an accurate call. If you tend to "overset" or "trap set," cover your hitter or pull back on defense to dig the opponent hitting the overset. The setter is usually the first to know that her set will be unhittable and consequently is in the best position to dig the blocked ball. There is nothing quite like covering a blocked ball and transitioning it into another point-scoring opportunity.

Covering a blocked ball is deflating to the opponent and uplifting for the scoring team. Too often, the setter is watching the flight of the ball and not repositioning herself to cover the hitter. Moving to cover and looking at the opponents' defense can be done at the same time by the setter—it just has to be practiced.

Setting the end-line pass

When one teammate is served deep to the back of the court, the job of the setter is to give a high enough forward set that provides the hitter time to get to the ball. This means that the setter has to not only adjust the set height for her partner but the depth of the set from the net. A set that is on top of the net or just a few feet back is difficult to hit when the starting point is the back of the court. A better choice is a set three to four feet off the net along with an accurate shot call.

Setting from a short serve

Earlier in this book, I explained that serving short is a good strategy because most passers will pass too tight, which in turn doesn't allow room for a partner to set the ball well. When a passer passes a short serve she has to take care to pull the pass back, off the net, to allow her partner enough room to set effectively. In addition to passing off the net, the pass needs to be higher to allow enough time for her to back up and make a full approach. The setter must always attempt to give the hitter enough set height to have a full approach.

Height and location of the set

The height and location of the set should be dictated by the passer, who obviously will become the hitter. If the hitter does not ask for anything specific, the set location should be on a straight line to the net from where she is standing to start her approach. The hitter will usually get a better set if she tells the setter the location and height of the set she wants instead of having the setter guess. For example, "I'm with you"—Interpretation: "Don't push the set to me, I'll come to you." Another example, "push it out"—Interpretation: "Set me to the sideline." Hitters can also ask for height variations as well. If hitters ask for a "low" or "quick" set, they are probably trying to do one of three things: beat the block, hit a lower set due to the wind, or a partner is simply setting too high. Each time hitters ask for what they want with the set, they help the setter improve the quality of the set they receive. The pass/set combinations are as numerous as the indoor game—even though most sand teams will hit the same set height in the same location time and time again.

Back sets

As mentioned, there are more options for hitters than just hitting the same set all the time; hitting a back set is a great option to vary the offense. When should a team hit a back set? First, a back set can be very effective when facing slow blocks as they may not chase you to the other half of the court. Secondly, it can be used to tire the blocker who needs to travel a great distance to the net. Another reason to use the back set is to change the attack zone of the hitter and to make the defense adjust to a hitter hitting from a zone they have not previously seen from the attacker. Finally, the best reason to hit a back set is to simply hit from the better half of the court (hit into the wind). All of these are good reasons to get comfortable calling and setting back sets. When there is a significant wind advantage on one half of the court (wind blowing from sideline to sideline, not from end line to end line), hitting from the good half can make siding out easier. For example, if the left side player is on the bad half of the court, she can ask for a set behind her partner and hit from the right side (even though she was served on the left). It is easier to hit into the wind from the good half of the court because the ball is blowing to the hitter's arm instead of away from it, assuming the left side hitter is right-handed. When actually spiking into the wind, the hitter can be more effective because the wind will keep the spike in and the ball drops quickly as well, which makes it hard to dig. The difficulty with the back set is quality control.

When the hitter calls for a back set, the setter must make an immediate adjustment; she must quickly turn her shoulders to square up to the opposite side of the court to set the back set. There simply isn't time to turn around and face where she is setting. This can be very challenging, but if a partner can give verbal cues while she has her back to the setting area it will help with location and height. Back sets add a dimension to any offense and can really help, not only in the wind but to potentially have a blocker pull instead of following the hitter. When blockers pull, they may be significantly weaker on defense and now the hitter has an attractive attack target—the pulling blocker.

Setting off the net

On the beach, the preferred set is about two feet off the net. At times, that distance may be even further to deal with a big block or to force your opponent to have to decide either to stay or pull and play down defense. By setting the ball off the net, it gives the hitter a chance to better deal with a big blocker or an open net to attack if the blocker pulls. The second reason is to give a bigger hitter the opportunity to swing without netting and increase hitting range. Tall players need a set that is off unless the strategy is to hit over the block, which a hitter with a big jump or high reach can do. Hitters are stubborn; they think that a "right on" set is the set they need to put the ball straight down and as a player I had the same perspective.

As a coach I have seen this much too often—players want their sets on the net but they don't realize that they are so much more effective with a set slightly off the net. When a set is tight the hitter usually gets blocked or nets. Either way the chances for success decrease. And the outlook is not that positive.

The "code"

In the indoor game, the offense is based on signals from the setter that are indicators as to what each hitter is going to hit. On the beach, each partner will need to have a code for their sets—something that can be flexible and verbal depending on how the play develops. My definition of a code is a simple selection of words that hitters can say to describe the set they want in the fewest words possible. In beach volleyball, every time a team is on offense there can be a variety of options for the hitters. They can hit a high set at the antenna, an inside set, a back set, a back wide set, a quick, and so on. Creating a code (short descriptive words to describe the set height and location the hitter wants) can make the setting call quick, efficient, and personalized for any program or team.

A team I coached used the colors of the rainbow to describe the location and height of the sets. It was important to them not to yell out "high outside" and announce to their opponents what they intended to hit but to have a code that would indicate what set they wanted. Red, for instance, was the standard set—not too high, not too wide. Pink was a quick set to the antenna, and so on. In a strong partnership each will take the time to understand the other's verbal cues. It is very important to be clear about each other's intentions. "I'm with you" might have two different meanings from two different partners. The code doesn't have to be sophisticated but it can be a fun team-building exercise for a new partnership. College programs can standardize their sets and each member of the team will use the terminology or code that the coach or players create.

Setting separates the good teams from the average. The second contact is typically the "fix the problem" contact. In volleyball, just about every contact is in some way an error correction. This is exaggerated with the set. A poor set puts the whole point-scoring opportunity in jeopardy whether it's serve receive or a dig. Think of the possibilities that accurate setting offers—an opportunity to hit with the best vision, to build trust for the team, and to reduce stress on the passer to be perfect.

©John Bartelt

Liz Masakayan

7 OFFENSIVE TACTICS

On the beach, teams try to keep their offense simple—high sets to the same position over and over again. This approach is necessary since most teams bump set and do not use their hands as explained in Chapter 6. The most effective teams can "see" defenders and either make them run down shots or simply use their power to bang the ball to the ground. It's completely different than the indoor game where there are multiple offensive plays and up to four players to involve in the offense. It's obvious who is going to get set on the beach—the person who receives the serve. Because of this, sometimes teams lack creativity in their offense. The options are many, even if it is obvious who is going to get set. Hitters can choose to hit from different areas of the net, hit a variety of set heights, and hit a variety of types of shots. When the ball is on your side of the court, you are in charge of making their defense work hard to dig you, not just hold and pursue. Keeping it simple works if you are just too overpowering for them to dig or block. But, for average players we need as much help as we can get. Having more in your offensive pocket also gives you the ability to better handle difficult wind conditions as well. If you have used a lower set, run back sets, or hit from the middle in previous matches, it becomes easier to find solutions during difficult situations at match time. Make the blocker move, make the defender make adjustments, hit from the middle, hit from the antenna, hit a set off the net, and most of all, don't be predictable.

Hitters who take a look at the defense, while in the loading position just before jumping during their approach, will have a huge advantage over those hitters who only see the block. Looking at the defender behind the block makes you less dependent on a good call from your partner for your shot selections. Learning the head bob is different than seeing the block as the hitter. Looking at the defense and not being dependent on a good call is a huge advantage, and almost all great players utilize this skill. Experienced indoor players who have adapted to the beach game will automatically see the block in front of them and deduce that the shot over the block is probably open. But just because you see what is in front of you doesn't mean you are not being set up for an easy dig. I'll expand on this further in the section on defense.

As stated earlier, the setters should be looking at the defense and calling the open areas but they can be wrong, late, or worse yet, forgetful. Hitters who take a look at the defender are frustrating to defend because the defender knows they see their base starting area and that, of course, is an advantage to the offense. Seeing the defender becomes more important the longer the rally goes on. Why? Because the more fatigued the defenders get, the less likely they are to maintain a structured defense and holes in the court are created. These gaps in their defense, the result of fatigue from the long rally, provide opportunity for the hitter—if she's watching. It is important that hitters take advantage of the gaps that appear in the defense, but hitters can't exploit the holes if they don't look to see where where the defenders are on the court.

The head bob

There are two different ways a hitter can look at the offense—the "head bob" which is used to see the defenders behind the block and the "peripheral look" to see the block. I teach all of the players I coach to always use the "head bob" as you cannot be a top player without being able to look at the down defender or, in some cases, both of the defenders. This look at the defense occurs before they jump. The head bob gives you an opportunity to look at the opponent's back court defender at the precise time you are preparing to jump to hit (the last two steps of the approach just before takeoff). This look at the defense occurs before they jump. I smile when I see players take three looks at the defender prior to jumping to hit. I tell them it's all old information by the time they jump because the defender has readjusted. Unless hitters can jump extremely high and beat every block and hit so powerfully that they cannot be dug, the best and most effective way to score is by looking and hitting where the defender isn't covering.

The head bob is also useful when playing against a two-down defense because the hitter can find the open areas of the court or see where the weaker partner is playing on defense. This gap, or open area of the court, is extremely valuable information. A setter can yell the wrong shot selection but if hitters can look and take care of their own hitting choices, they have one more asset at their disposal.

Telegraphing

Telegraphing is defined as "to make known in advance, intentional or unintentional, especially with body language." Therefore, to "telegraph" your hit is to unintentionally let the defender know what you mean to do on your attack. Defenders are looking at the body language of the hitter and reading the information prior to reacting to best anticipate the hitter's hit. The best defenders don't watch the ball until the last moment. Knowing this is the case, hitters should try to make every approach look the same and not telegraph their hit. I train players to be hitters first and shooters second because hitters force defenders to stay in their defensive base position longer. A defender's first responsibility is to dig the hard driven ball and secondly run down the shot. Great hitters keep the defense in the dark about the shot for as long as possible by always taking an aggressive approach and then, at the last moment, slowing down their arm and hitting a shot. Turning in the air to face line, straightening an arm, dropping an elbow, and closing a hand are all forms of telegraphing the hitter's intentions. If every approach is full speed and looks like the hitter can swing crosscourt, then it forces the defender to hold for the hit longer—which is the key to not giving the defenders a head start to run down a shot.

Covering

As a player, I was always of the mindset that the block should be avoided at all costs. Fortunately, I could jump high enough that I could hit over or around most blocks, but never would I have deliberately hit into the block with the intention of self-covering. I have since seen something done by players on tight sets that I think is a great emergency play—the deliberate hit into the block. The player hits an off-speed spike directly into the block with the sole intention of covering herself and giving the team another swing. This typically is done on a tight set and is a great way to take the wind out of the sails of the blocker. Hit the shot easy into the block and be prepared to pass the covered ball to your partner. Remember, nobody covers you like you, so be ready to cover any ball you hit into the block yourself, or work on making sure that your teammate will be prepared to cover you.

Shot options

The "waterfall" is an off-speed shot short over the block or short in front of a deep defender on a two-down defense. The waterfall can also be effective if a blocker pulls angle as it drops short line and is difficult for the down defender to dig. The waterfall is an arching shot that just clears the block yet falls deep enough to be out of reach of the blocker and the defender—like a little waterfall over the block. It is confusing as to whose ball it is, the defender or the landing blocker, which makes it effective.

Kathy Gregory, long time UCSB Women's volleyball coach and beach volleyball legend, coined the term "jumbo shrimp" for a deep arching shot that goes over the down defender's head and lands deep crosscourt in the corner. The shot is difficult to play due to its location and difficult to read because it freezes defenders in their tracks. The jumbo shrimp is very effective during a long rally when defenders get closer and closer to the net. Note, this shot is very difficult to learn and takes training but is well worth the investment in time and repetition training.

High tool

The high tool is not just for line attacks! Unlike the deliberate hit into the block, the high tool is a hit that is actually aiming for the hands of the blocker with the intention of not getting blocked and making the ball unplayable or out of bounds. This shot is intentionally hit upward to hit the fingertips of the block, not the hands of the blocker. To execute the high tool, hitters can use a full-force swing as long as they swing high, not down. The key is to keep the elbow high. Be aware, smart blockers who have constantly been tooled will pull their hands and the hit can sail out of bounds untouched.

Hitting from center

Most players are comfortable hitting a moderately high set somewhere in front of wherever they received the serve. Typically, this choice of set gives them the most open court on their crosscourt attack (the easier swing). Redundancy can make the hitter predictable. The hitter should, if possible, move their sets around with their ball control and setting skills. A great option is to hit from the middle. Hitting a set from the center of the court can provide an opportunity to change things up and force the defense to commit to one side or the other of the blocker. For the defense, the question is if the attacker is in the center and the plan was to block line, what is being blocked now that the hitter is attacking from the middle?

This little edge for the offense can be very useful as it is likely that the defense has not previously discussed the middle defense strategy plan. Later in her career, Elaine Youngs elected to hit the majority of her sets from the middle. Elaine would simply chip the ball into one of the four corners of the court and was rarely dug, but if the blocker pulled, she would swing away. The middle set makes defenders commit to a defensive position that is usually to one side or another of the block so they can have a visual on the hitter's shoulders. The setter for the offense can take a look and call the open side of the court, and a short or deep chip shot to the open half of the court is very effective and hard to pursue for the defender. Defensively, blockers can help neutralize this middle attack chip shot by pulling off the net late and short to help take a portion of the court.

For the offense, if the defense begins to play short for the chip shots it opens up all of the deep areas of the court.

Hitting from all zones of the net

I am a firm believer that a hitter should be able to hit from all areas of the net and hit a variety of set heights. Hitting from the antenna is a great way to open up the court and provide an opportunity to tool the block into the antenna. When I coached Jennifer Kessy and April Ross, we had a training session with a couple of men they knew. The drill was that Jen and April had to hit the line, shoot the line, or tool the line blocker—only line was available in the drill. The men they were training with heard the parameters of the drill and could do anything they liked to defend them. The men mixed up blocking line, giving line, and even double covering the line. Jen and April were brilliant at this drill. What they did best was set the ball to the pin, tool the block, or if the block gave them line, the team mixed up using a waterfall, deep line mixed in with hard driven hits. They won the drill without hitting a single crosscourt ball.

Hitting from a variety of areas on the net is great, but another option is to lower the set. Hitting a low set can help the hitter beat the blocker who is running up to block after a serve. It also helps with increased ball control on windy days because keeping the set low reduces the amount it will blow in the wind. Sometimes hitting a lower set can help out a hitter who is experiencing timing issues and keeps getting under the set. When I played with Karrie Poppinga late in my career, we had a set that was similar to a slow indoor three set that we called the "whooee." We used this set so I could beat the blocker and it was a fun way to pick up our tempo during a rally. It was also easy for us because we used our hand set instead of bump setting, which is always more accurate and easier to direct. Experimenting with this is not only fun but adds a lot of variety to a team's offense.

Setting off the net

As mentioned earlier, setting the ball three or four feet off the net into what I call the "should they stay or should they go zone" is a good tactic because the blocker doesn't always know what the right move is with an off set. It can also be a great location for a bigger hitter. I have coached several very tall athletes who were actually more effective hitting an offset because of their long reach and good jump. The set off the net actually gave them greater range as a hitter. It's funny—most players are very stubborn and will fight any idea of a set off the net. The setter resists, the hitter resists, and I most always had a very tough time selling the concept to players I've coached. I understand. As a player, I would never want a set off the net, but as a coach, you simply see things differently and understand how much more effective the hitter can be with a set that isn't on top of the net or even just one foot back. Smaller players can also benefit from not having a tight set because an offset will make a big blocker pull, which puts a big blocker in a down defensive position. A big blocker on the ground is much easier to beat than a big blocker facing a tight set. I'm a firm believer in hitting at retreating blockers and forcing them to have to dig, which is probably not their number-one skill.

Making the blocker cover more distance

One strategy a hitter can use on serve receive is to make the blocker move as far as possible along the net to block. For example, if a player is served line to line the hitter can ask for a wide back set and make the blocker run further to get to the hitter. Every additional step in the sand adds up, especially as the match goes on. When serving, a primary blocker who is forced to run the diagonal distance to the net is going to run a further distance than if she only has to run straight forward to the net. This extra distance can create a weaker blocking situation—the blocker might not be able to get there in time to block, or later in the match, decide not to make the effort to chase the hitter and just pull off. If blockers are jump serving, the momentum of the server gets them to the net quicker but there is a way to beat them—run a back wide, low-shoot set to the antenna. Frequently, blockers will not pursue a distant set and will decide to pull off the net instead. This will then give the hitter a target on the ground rather than a blocker in her face.

Overthinking

What makes a hitter overthink? Frustration. It is frustrating to get blocked repetitively, get dug time and time again, or to continually receive poor sets. All lead to overthinking. When a hitter is worrying about what the defender behind the blocker is doing, or if the blocker is staying or pulling, or the inconsistency of the set, these can all add up to "paralysis by analysis" which is what I call overthinking. Overthinking can cause unforced hitting errors or worse, passing errors. When stuck in the situation described above, players can get themselves out by trying some of the following tricks:

1. Hit a back set.
2. Hit a lower set.
3. Hit deep middle to the opponent.
4. Switch sides with their partner.

All of these variations give the hitter a different perspective and relieve some of the stress created by overthinking.

Offense is the most enjoyable part of playing the game of beach volleyball for me. I received satisfaction in having the ability to hit from the middle, back sets, from the antenna, or a quick set when available. This flexibility I believe extended my career greatly, especially when I was less healthy in the later years. Hitting from the same old spot is boring and predictable. Taking charge of your game by learning to look at the defense (the head bob) and having the confidence to hit from different areas of the net expands your ability to be successful on offense. Keep in mind that, when necessary, hitting into the block intentionally (and remembering to cover yourself) can also be an effective way to restart the play if you are given a tight set. Disguising what you are doing is as important as being able to execute the shot or hit. Come in for every approach like you are going to swing away—never use a slow, shooter's approach. Relax and keep your mind clear, and remember there is always an open area on the court. Your job is to find it.

Lisa Rutledge-Fitzgerald blocking, Brooke Niles on defense

8 Effective Blocking

In beach volleyball whatever the plan may be, the flexibility to change that plan during the match is critical. The luxury of having a player or players who are effective blockers can certainly make team defense more interesting and fun. In this chapter I will discuss the choices that blockers make to either block angle, line, or the cut and when to pull line, angle, to the cut or short line. The hardest part about blocking is the decision to stay or pull off the net based on the location of the set or effectiveness of the hitter. I watched Kerri Walsh Jennings do something at the 2016 Olympics in Rio that reasserts the importance of fake blocking and pulling. In the second set of the first round of pool play, Kerri pulled angle three times in a row against Mariafe Artacho del Solar from Australia. Consequently Mariafe hit into the net twice and was easily dug once. Again, later in that same match, Kerri pulled line late and Mariafe hit the ball out long for a point. All of this action was after Kerri had blocked her for numerous points in the first set. Kerri mixed it up, frustrated her opponent, and absolutely got into her head.

The positioning and timing of the blocker are equally as important when deciding whether you should remain up and block. A blocker who recognizes the importance of setting the block correctly and the timing of when to jump is of course more effective than a blocker whose positioning and/or timing is off. The strategy of when to apply a particular blocking scheme or pulling options are certainly part of learning how to best use your team's strengths or exploit your opponent's weaknesses. Each level of blocking that you can rise to and experiment with adds a new dimension to your defense and provides solutions to even the toughest offense.

Back in the early 1970s blockers were not allowed to penetrate over the net and most women didn't block. In the 1980s the rules changed and so did the game. Blocking became an instrumental part of the game and most teams had a primary blocker (someone who served and ran up to block and that player also blocked in transition). The first women on the beach to become primary blockers were mostly over six feet tall. There were also the jumpers—me, Liz Masakayan, and Jackie Sylvia—who were five feet eight inches but had the hang time necessary to be successful blockers. I always enjoyed the blocking role and only late in my career did I become a primary defender. There is nothing quite like getting a stuff block, directing the team on how to defend a hitter, and making quick blocking decisions at the net. I remember the last tournament I won as a professional in 1996. I was in Long Beach and on match point I had a stuff block—a very satisfying moment, especially considering that I was still bummed I did not make the Olympic team for Atlanta. In a standard set up, the blocker blocks either line or angle and tries to eliminate a hard-driven spike to a designated portion of the court, somewhat freeing up the defender's responsibility. Blockers communicate this by holding up fingers behind their back so they are hidden from the opponent but in sight of the serving partner. The right hand pertains to the opponent's left-side player and the left hand pertains to the right-side player. The most common signals are one finger for blocking line and two fingers for blocking angle. Here are a few examples:

1. One finger—blocking and pulling line.

2. Two fingers—blocking angle and pulling angle.

3. First and fourth fingers of one hand—blocking line on both players and pulling line.

4. One finger with movement or flashing—blocking line, pulling angle.

5. Fist—blocking ball and can sometimes mean pulling.

6. Open hand and closing hand—pulling no matter what (other than over set).

7. One hand high—serving target, lower hand is the block assignment. For example, high hand is a two and lower hand is a one. Translation is serve area two and I'm blocking line on that player you are serving. Using this signal system is a great way to tell your partner who to serve and what to block as well.

8. Four fingers—blocking crosscourt and pulling to the cut.

There are several ways the blocker can do more for the team and put more stress on the opponent's offense. Depending on what the defense is trying to take away from a team or give a team on offense, those decisions can work to contain the hitter's choices. Unfortunately, not every team has the luxury of having a player who can block effectively and the teams without strong blocking will need to play a "two-down defense."

Olympians Shelda Bede and Adriana Behar from Brazil played on the FIVB tour for ten years without a tall blocker. Shelda was five feet five inches tall, and Adriana was about five feet ten inches. Adriana did all the blocking. Several taller Brazilian players tried to lure Shelda away, but combined talent were extremely effective and they remained a team for years. They won more FIVB World Tour gold medals than any other team in the history of beach volleyball, as well as two Olympic silver medals in 2000 and 2004 and more than a million dollars in prize money. However, if there is a player able to do the job of the blocker, or if both players will split block (share blocking responsibilities), then the blocking strategy should be discussed prior to the match so both players are on the same page.

In beach volleyball the flexibility to change the blocking plan during the match is critical. The team needs to have the ability to continuously adjust their blocking to the particulars of the opponents' offense during the match.

Deciding how to make the blocking assignments should be based on several factors. What are the hitter's strengths? Should the blocker block line or angle? Would an occasional dive block work? If they are constantly shooting the ball over the block can your team delay block or pull? Does the hitter have an effective cut that is hard to stop? If so, can you block the cut shot or pull to the cut? Is the hitter constantly hitting a waterfall shot and would pulling short be effective? How is the wind affecting the hitting tendencies of the opponent and how can you use the wind to help your defense?

Teams should determine the need for their blocking assignments from one of the following informational sources:

1. **Previous knowledge of the opponent.** Has either partner previously played with one or both of the opponents and knows their strengths and weaknesses? If so, they should use that information as part of their blocking game plan.

2. **Watching the opponent play.** Players and/or coaches should take time to scout the opponent prior to the match whether on video, or better yet live, if at all possible. When scouting, is the defensive plan being used against your opponent working and if so, can your team do the same? What are the patterns of the hitters? Who are they serving and is it effective? What can your team do better? Taking mental or written notes about who to serve and what was effective and ineffective is valuable information to help prepare defensive plans.

3. **Team strengths.** A tall but less-agile blocker may need to stick to line blocking and do less angle blocking or ball blocking due to reduced speed and effectiveness

when moving. Also, a quick or experienced defender may want to gamble more on defense than someone who is less experienced. There are teams that split block early in the match or early in the tournament. They do this to rest the primary blocker for later matches due to fitness or heat concerns.

4. **Blocking each the player's line**. This is the simplest plan and the best if there is no specific reason to do something different.

Line blocking

Taking line, as a blocker, means you are blocking the hard-driven ball that is a hit attack down the sideline of the attacker. By the blocker taking the line, the first responsibility of the defender is digging the hard-driven crosscourt hit. The defender's secondary responsibility is to run down the shot. The shot may be a high shot over the line blocker, a deep angle shot over the defender (jumbo shrimp), or a cut shot that is cross court sharp along the net. The top defenders believe that any hit ball can be touched and will always be pursued. Barbara Fontana, Nick Lucena, Holly McPeak, Brooke Niles, Todd Rogers, and other great defenders all have the "never quit" attitude and will make an effort to touch anything that gets around the block.

Dive blocking

The principle behind dive blocking (aka "bait blocking") is that you are showing the hitter the area with your body position and jumping into the opposite area of the net from where you are starting your base blocking position. Obviously, to do this well you need to be proficient at area blocking, very tall, or have a great vertical jump! One of the first women to do this effectively was Olympian Elaine Youngs, who had both height and a good jump. Elaine had fantastic instincts and was especially effective against those who preferred to swing, as opposed to shooting the ball. Dive blocking is most effective when used sporadically; you don't want the hitter to become accustomed to the last moment switching of the blocker's assignment and make adjustments. If timed correctly, dive blocking can create doubt in the hitter. Doubt hurts confidence. Most players use this technique to jump into the angle, but I have see success with dive blocking into the line as well. Line dive blocking is a bit less effective since the hitter can tool the block into the antenna. Dive blocking into the angle will not typically allow for a tool into the antenna.

The upside of dive/bait blocking:

- Dive blocking adds another dimension to defensive game plans as it makes calling the shot area difficult. The call cannot be made exclusively from the defender's starting position.
- The hitter is not expecting the block to jump into the open "swing" area of the court. If hitters choose to not challenge the block but instead to hit to the open/given area, they can be stuffed-blocked for a point.

The downside of dive/bait blocking:

- The blocker loses height and penetration on the block, and without proper penetration, the blocker can be tooled.

- Both partners need to be in sync with the plan or it puts the defender out of position.

Delay blocking/shot blocking

Sometimes players are so effective shooting the ball over the block, blockers need to either pull off the net, play down defense, or wait on the ground and jump late to swat the shot in midair. The most critical aspect of this technique is to practice it during training sessions prior to using it for the first time during a match. Delaying on the ground prior to jumping and making a quick, explosive jump is the key. In addition to having great instincts, blockers also may need to use their arms independently to extend their ability to reach the slower-moving shots. By potentially using one hand to reach for a slow-moving shot, a blocker can cover more area and be more effective. The risk that a shot blocker takes is that the opponent will recognize the delay and swing quickly, thus nullifying the blocker as a defensive element. This approach is best used when a player is in "shot mode" and is continuously and effectively shooting over the block.

Blocking the cut shot

The blocker has two choices when an opponent has such an effective cut shot that it seems impossible to defend on the ground. First, the blocker can pull to the cut late, and the second is to shot block the cut. The key to shot blocking the cut is to take a step to the inside of the court at the last moment to intercept the ball further down the net. Baiting the hitter into this shot is important because if the hitter keys into this early, the defense (by seeing an early step from the blocker or an early commitment from the down defender) is very vulnerable to a short line shot or a hard middle hit.

Blocking in the wind

Liz Masakayan is a great strategic coach and a player who really understood the effect of wind on the sand game. Liz knew how the wind could force players to hit a particular shot or how it would affect the set quality. On windy days she thought about how the windy conditions would affect the opponent's offensive hitting locations. For example, if the wind was blowing through the end line at a significant speed and Liz's team was on the good side (wind in her team's face), she would remind the blocker that the ball is going to blow on the net, and the blocker should stay and block rather than pull off the net. Conversely, when the team switched sides, Liz would remind her partner that the wind is going to blow the set off and that they will be doing more pulling than blocking.

Another example is a side-court wind. Typically on the Pacific coast, the wind blows onshore and slightly north to south. The team on the south side of a north/south facing court is going to want the right side player to hit angle, or into the wind. The left side player is going to want to hit or shoot line, also into the wind. Offensively, the right-side player hitting a line shot runs the risk of having the shot blown out of bounds. The left-side player, due to the scenario described, usually has a difficult time hitting crosscourt because the ball is being blown away from her hitting arm and runs the risk of being blown out of bounds wide.

What can blockers do to set up a successful defensive strategy in these conditions? Blockers can take what they know the hitter does not want to hit so the hitter will feel comfortable swinging away from the blocker. In other words, the blocker, when blocking a right-side player (who wants to avoid a hitting error on her sideline due to the wind blowing the ball out), takes her line so she is free to hit what she wants—angle. Your defender will be there to pick up the shot or to dig the hit, or defensively the team can do the opposite—double up on the angle by blocking and digging the crosscourt hit/shot. With the left-side player, block crosscourt to allow her to swing and hit the line (her preferred hitting choice due to strong wind) and you have put the defender to cover line.

The opposite would take place on the side switch—block angle on the right-side player and block line on the left. The defense is trying to encourage the opponent to hit the obvious shot in these particular wind conditions, and set up defense so they are in the best position to dig a ball the hitter wants to hit.

Pulling

The choice to pull off the net and not block can be based on the quality of the set the hitter receives or the perceived strength of the hitter. I was playing in a match on a very hard surface in New Orleans and at that time

I was playing against my friend Liz. She was recovering from one of her knee surgeries and I thought, on a particular set, that I should pull off the net and play down defense. Liz, however, played her usual aggressive game and unloaded her spike which struck me smack in my face. Liz hit a very heavy ball and it was a solid facial. Unfortunately, I did not learn my lesson and again, later in the match, I pulled and she once again hit me so hard in the face with the ball that the color from the ball was imprinted onto my glasses and my face was bleeding. As an important safety tip, make sure you are ready to defend the hitter, and if she can hit as well as Liz, it's best not to drop off the net.

Most blockers tend to pull off the net when choosing not to block to their call (the side of the court they were blocking). The most common is if they are blocking line and the set is off, they pull line. If the call was angle, then the pull is angle. It can be much more sophisticated than this based on hitter tendencies, wind, defensive strategies, or even just a gut feeling. Signals to your partner can be developed to communicate a variety of pulls. They can be a simple line/angle pull or something you have to indicate a more elaborate pull based on wind conditions or a particular hitter's tendencies.

There are four types of blocking pulls: pulling line, pulling crosscourt, pulling short line, and pulling to the cut. The safest and most productive is pulling line as it is the shortest distance to a reasonable defensive spot and most hitters will prefer their angle hit on an open net. Also the stationary defender is usually in a better position to dig more area.

Pulling Short

Retired AVP professional Carrie Dodd is an exceptional athlete. She could be both a primary blocker (although small at five feet eleven inches) or a great down defender. What Carrie perfected was a move where she would make a late pull short on tight sets, which usually equaled an easy short shot pickup for her. Carrie realized early on in her career that when she was blocking tight sets, players would often try to "poke" the ball over the block short instead of battle at the net. Carrie would make a late "short pull" in anticipation of the hitter poking the ball short. This technique would not be good for an aggressive hitter that swings on tight sets, but a very useful strategy for smaller players and smaller blockers.

Faking the pull

Another way to shake up the predictability of the block is to fake a pull and then return to block. This is especially effective after the blocker has repeatedly pulled or if the opponent looks at the court early and can see you making a pull move and thinks the net is open. The key to this strategy is the sale of the fake and the effectiveness of the return up to block. The gamble is the hitter will attack with a swing at the supposed pulling blocker, so when the blocker returns, she needs to take line (because most people pull line and the hitter will typically hit line to attack a late-retreating blocker).

Blocking or faking the block adds an additional dimension to any defensive strategy and should be fully utilized beyond the typical line/angle blocking pattern. Combining different blocking schemes to combat the opponent's offense is a fun and rewarding way to score defensive points. Practicing dive blocking, fake blocking, bait blocking, cut-shot blocking, as well as all of the varieties of pulling, takes time and many repetitions. The first time you block a cut shot, or pull short and easily pick up a short poke shot, or fake a pull and get a stuff block, will make all the training and preparation seem like an excellent investment of your time.

Brooke Niles

9 DEFENSIVE VARIATIONS

Defense is the chess game of beach volleyball and to be a good defender requires dedication, patience, and most importantly, spirit. As Liz Masakayan so clearly phrased it, "You've got to get the defender to sit their ass down, then use your shots." Good defenders make defense look easy. To the casual eye, it appears that the hitter is actually trying to hit the ball to the defender as she always seems to be in the right place at the right time, or simply a step or two away from the ball. The inside game that is going on to create that illusion is one of the more interesting aspects of beach volleyball. We can never actually tell what is going on in the minds of our opponents, but we are always trying to anticipate their next move. That's what defense is: anticipation and preparation. I've always loved the quote "no brains, no headaches" because sometimes our brain does get in the way of our athletic flow. In the case of defense, it is about our brain, heart, instincts, and a good memory. The trickery of setting up a dig is the challenge. How to best implement some of the great tips that follow in this chapter will be fun and hopefully provide some variety in your defensive arsenal.

The standard "base" position on defense in serve receive or in transition is slightly off the inside shoulder of the blocker, her butt to the corner of the court about eight to ten feet from the corner of the court and stationary. How far into the court defenders hold is based on their strengths; a taller player may begin shallower in the court because she can protect deep hits with an overhead dig and may not be as quick moving forward. Smaller or very quick players may elect to start deeper as they trust their speed and can quickly get the shorter hits or shots. The most common defensive scheme is to block line and run down the line shot. Such a base position puts the defender in the most advantageous location to do this. When running baseline defense, the first priority and responsibility of the defender is to dig the hard-driven angle spike and the blocker's responsibility is to take away the hard-hit line. If the set is off the net, the blocker, unless previously discussed or indicated by a signal, will pull back defensively to the sideline from where the hitter was to be hitting from. When the blocker does pull off the net, the down defender has the middle hit and everything else crosscourt. The retreat blocker protects everything on her sideline.

The juke

The gamesmanship of beach volleyball begins with what you can do to create defensive advantages. I like to think of defense as a chess match between teams and the "juke" is one of the first level moves in beach volleyball. Juking is an exaggerated defensive movement to try and fool the opponents setter to call the wrong shot call for their hitter. If the juke is successful and the opponent buys the fake out, the result is an easy dig for the defender. Juking is not useful at the very beginning levels as neither the hitter nor the setter looks at what the opponent is doing so there would be no benefit to juking to fool them—they aren't paying attention! Juking can be a very effective tactic if it isn't overused and if it doesn't interfere with the defenders' ability to play defense. If a player does juke, the important thing is to get stationary and prepared to react just before the hitter's contact. Once an opponent is onto the defender's juke, a fake juke (going to the actual direction you are faking) is an additional strategy to experiment with. It is really fun to see how you can trick someone with your body movements, but sometimes being too tricky can backfire if the defender is never stationary for the hit or won't pursue a shot ball.

The creep

The creep is a slow, deliberate movement to show the opponent that you are sliding into the assigned spot you should be on defense. For example, the blocker is taking line and the defender's primary assignment on defense would be to dig the crosscourt spike or get the cut. Let's say my blocker is blocking line and I want to "pretend" to be sneaking into the crosscourt, thus creeping. However, I am doing this deliberately with the intention of running down the "shot," which is line, as soon as the hitter goes to hit. The defender is trying to get noticed so that the opponent's setter yells to the hitter, "line." The actual intention of the defender is to be noticed so the opponent's setter or hitter, if they look, sees them doing this action. The hitter thinks, "Oh, I totally see them on my angle. I'll shoot the line." The hitter's partner confirms this by seeing the defender on their angle and calls, "line!" The defender all along has no intention of actually staying crosscourt, but wants to bait the hitter to shoot the ball line. Once the hitter is in the air, the defender runs to the shot, which was the intention all along. The obvious risk is that the hitter doesn't shoot the ball over the block but elects to hit and the defender is caught on the move. That is a chess move that has to be well thought out. If the hitter doesn't look before hitting, and the setter doesn't give the hitter a call, this would not be a tactic to use. The creep, if used sparingly, can be an effective way to get a dig for a momentum change. This technique, coupled with some of the others mentioned in this section, provides a variety of scenarios to confuse the opponent's offensive caller (the setter) or the looker (hitter taking care of her shot selection).

Showing and taking away

An option for the defender is to make an early and obvious base defense shift (instead of the slow creep), while planning on moving from that area to the "open" area that was left unattended. For example, the defender makes an early move to dig the line while planning to run down the cut shot. The caller sees you standing for a dig line and calls "cut!" (shot over the block), and the defender sprints to the ball after hearing the call. Defensively, this will set the stage of hitter doubt (if done correctly and successfully), which is a huge team advantage to gain. The hitter is left to wonder if the defender will stay or go and the setter is wondering the same thing when making the call for the hitter. When a hitter is overthinking, it isn't a good state of mind for them to be in—thinking too much inhibits getting into a groove or flow. Again, strategically timed defensive plays are better used on occasion, as the best defenders read the hitter, are stationary at the hitter's contact, and react to all the events leading up to the hit.

Doubling up

Doubling up on a hitter means that you are blocking and digging the same area. Doubling up can be very effective if the hitter is queuing her shot choice based on the blocker's position (shooting line if blocking line, hitting the cut when blocking the angle). This defense will not work if the hitter's partner calls the correct area of the court and the hitter listens. Fortunately for the defenders, many hitters do not listen to their setter's call, but "see" the block and hit or shoot accordingly. It is a great one-off play that can be a momentum changer if done at the proper time. It can also be effective if used against a hitter who does not possess certain hits. Why cover for a line hit when the hitter simply will not, or cannot, hit line? Play the percentages. Double up when necessary.

The "I" defense

There are times when a hitter constantly shoots to areas of the court that the defender is having trouble getting to—especially if the team runs their offense from the middle of the court. The "I" defense is when the blocker is blocking ball and the defender's starting position is directly behind the blocker, virtually hidden but not committed to either line or angle. The defender gives no indication which way she will break and her only goal is to get any shot on the court. This defensive scheme is frustrating to the offensive players because there is no clear call that the setter can give her partner. The setter (or the hitter if she does a head bob) sees the defender holding center and can only guess the most open area of the court. The blocker's primary responsibility is to take away the hitter's hard hit. If the blocker does not do this, the "I" formation is a weak defensive starting point to dig a hard-driven ball. Sometimes it is necessary to make changes if the team is having little or no successes in the standard defensive formations. No risk, no reward.

The game-opening shot or hit

I have played with and coached against players that have a favorite game-opening shot, and they will use this time and time again on their first attack of the match. Many times this hit or shot will be something that they want the defense to worry about for the entire match, but they don't use as much after the opening shot. Watch your opponents—if you find they have an opening game hit or shot, it can mean an easy first dig and point of the match. Make sure that the player with the opening shot tendency receives the first serve so your team can use this knowledge for a dig. This information, or the sharing of it, can quickly lead to the player hearing that people are aware of the habit and will quickly eliminate the opener. Keep this to yourself as you never know who your next partner will be.

Knowing your strengths

Understanding what you do best and knowing your weaknesses are key to becoming the best player you can be. For example, if you are very quick to move forward on defense but can't seem to turn and get balls over your head, a deeper starting position would play into your strengths. By positioning yourself deeper on base defense (closer to the sideline and end line), you put yourself in a position to run down shots and protect your weaknesses deep overhead because your starting position makes those shots easier to reach. Conversely, taller or slower players may have difficulty moving quickly to get a short cut shot. Their starting base defensive position would be up closer on defense (away from the sideline and end line) because they can protect shots overhead primarily due to their height (they can simply dig overhead instead of running down the ball like a smaller player may have to do).

Reading and experience

Players like Misty May-Treanor seem to always be in the right place at the right time and make defense look easy. But part of the reason Misty is so good is she grew up on the beach and had her dad, Butch May, to mentor her. Players who are new to the game of beach volleyball, or may not have grown up on the beach, need to acquire certain skills to be a great defender.

There is no substitute for experience, but there are shortcuts to the learning curve to better understand defense. First, knowing what hitters can't hit is as important as knowing what they can hit. Watch their warm up. Can they hit line? Do they have a decent cut? Is everything they hit hard angle? Taking notice can be a huge advantage as players usually have their go-to shots and hits, and playing the percentages certainly pays off defensively. They won't hit something they didn't even try in the warm up. Additionally, if they hit one high line shot the entire match, give it to them. Worrying about defending the once-a-match shot is a waste of energy. Let hitters have the shot they infrequently use and take all the rest away. Play for the highest percentage shot or hit and make your best effort to pursue every ball.

Reading the hitter's body language such as approach speed, arm swing, and shoulder turn are some of the first hints as to what the hitter may do. Defenders can get stuck watching the ball, the block, or possibly just worrying about what their assignment is as opposed to taking in all the relevant information.

Reading the hitter begins with understanding the hints given during their approach along with knowing what they like to hit. A slow approach usually equals a shot. A quick arm swing is a hit. A straight arm is usually a shot high line or a poke. If hitters open up their shoulders while hitting on the left, it's probably a cut shot. If hitters square up their shoulders, they are usually hitting line. Low elbow, straight elbow, look, no look, hard approach, slow approach—where is the ball in relationship to their body? What can't they hit with their body positioned the way it is? Paying attention to all the information given during the play can give defenders an advantage so they can dig more balls.

No block teams

The luxury of having a team with a player who is an outstanding blocker is not always possible. A team that plays without a blocker has some definite challenges, especially on a hard-packed sand court where players can pound the ball. When I was coaching indoor Olympian Tammy Leibl and Dianne DeNecochea in an AVP tournament in Sacramento, California, the sand was very hard packed and a very big advantage for Tammy and Dianne. They played a two-down team, the Lindquist sisters—Tracy and Katie. I've never seen balls bounced off the sand like that during a match, ever. The Lindquists could not defend the powerful offense of Tammy and Dianne, and it was utterly entertaining to watch them unload against a team without a block on a hard surface. But when it was at Huntington, or at other deep sand locations, the Lindquists covered the court expertly and frustrated many teams with their defensive skills. There are instances when having a partner who is an outstanding defender can be a better choice than a weak blocker. For example, on serve receive it would be better to have a partner who can set and effectively side out instead of a tall partner who can block but can't pass or set. Point scoring can be difficult without a block, but tough serving and tactical defense can be effective in overcoming a much larger team. Two-down defense is very common on public beaches and at recreational tournaments, but for college beach volleyball or the professional circuit, it would be next to impossible to be a champion due to the height and strength of the player's offense.

Playing against a two-down defense team can be very challenging to a small offensive team or an inexperienced team. What if the court appears balanced and no obvious gaps are available? Nonsense, something is always open. Have you considered the middle, short line, cut shot, jumbo shrimp or over the line defender deep? There are only two people and there is always something open—it just depends on how you look at their defense and what your options are.

I like this attacking sequence: first, hit deep middle, then if you score, the next hit is a cut (to keep the crosscourt defender from cheating to your middle hit). If she goes back to cheating to the cut shot, middle may be open or the line defender steps middle. If that happens, the short line is open. Once the line defenders play for the short line, deep line is open over their head. Some teams will pursue everything and never change their base defense; if that is the case, pick on the weaker hitter. Whoever digs becomes the hitter in transition. Serve that person too. Make this player have to work for everything and pretty soon she will become less effective during the match.

Psychology of the defender

Recognizing the patterns of the hitter is a talent that the best defenders acquire and develop during their career. Great defenders have a memory of past shots and patterns of their opponents and the ability to anticipate the future hit selection. These individuals are exceptional in their ability to keep a tally in their mind and many believe that every ball that clears the block is touchable by them on defense. The psychology of the top defender is that they are constantly learning about their opponent's tendencies and they NEVER GIVE UP. Defense is all about tenacity and constantly learning during the match.

The Rolodex

I was fortunate to coach 1996 Olympian Barbra Fontana after I retired from playing. I played against Barb for numerous years and always admired her tenacity and ability to be mentally tough and successful both on offense and defense. Barb was only five feet six inches tall but was an outstanding outside hitter at Stanford and a top beach player. When I coached Barb, she shared something about her game that I thought was brilliant. Barb kept a mental tally of player's hits and shots which she called their "Rolodex." A Rolodex is a small desktop filing system commonly used prior to computers. The Rolodex, for Barb, was the sequence in which players hit their shots. For example, when it came to players who Barbra knew well she might remember that they like to open the match with a high line shot followed by hitting hard angle as the second shot, then again back to high line, then to the cut, then the hard hit crosscourt and so on. She kept track of these tendencies and could anticipate which shot followed which (like flipping through the old-fashioned Rolodex). Barbra had a very high success rate due to paying attention to the player's Rolodex attacking order. In Barb's mind each individual has a personal Rolodex of shot or hit sequences. Although with the higher-level players, it is reasonable to anticipate that players receive good calls from their partners and the highest-level players look at the defense and hit it where the defender is most vulnerable.

Outstanding defenders need to remember not only the last shot/hit but how it affects the next hit. Players who are dug hard angle almost always will shoot line on the next hit (because they failed on the previous hit). Conversely, if players hit a high line shot and the defender doesn't even take a step, assume that they may "use it 'till they lose it" and continue with what is working until they are dug. I mentioned earlier in the book my coach, Dede Bodnar, had scouted an opponent for me prior to a professional match. She told me that the player had hit nothing but line shots. Of course, I didn't believe her and got burned on the first three shots this player hit down the line. I made an adjustment and dug the line and forced the player to hit a less comfortable hit for her, crosscourt. Dede was right and her observation skills were correct—the player did not change from one match to the next.

Baiting the hitter

Baiting hitters to hit their favorite shot, and the shot that you can dig as a defender, is another move of the chess match between offense and defense. Baiting the hitter involves timing and understanding the psychology of hitters. What is their favorite shot that they have the most confidence in? If your opponent's favorite shot is the cut, you can make this shot very attractive by starting your base position on defense shaded toward the line (with the blocker blocking line) knowing that as soon as the hitter makes contact you are sprinting to the cut for an easy dig. The bait is the huge area of the court you are giving the attacker, and knowing that they love the shot helps too! The defender dangles the open area only to know they are going to sprint there and the hitter takes the bait and hits the cut shot.

Giving it up now for the timely dig

Although it probably isn't the best plan to let a team continue to use a shot over and over again without defending the attack, there is something to be said about saving a particular dig for set point. Taking mental notes as to what has been working for the opponent is important. Just because you let the line shot fall the first five times doesn't mean you have to let it fall the sixth time. The opponent is also keeping track in her mind as to what has worked for her and it is very tempting to go to that shot during the highest-pressure moments. Frustration can be turned into opportunity if you stay focused! Remember what they like, take it away at the most opportune time, and turn frustration into success.

Taking away their favorite shot or hit—doubling up

Let's say that Jenny loves to hit angle. Your team has tried digging her but she continues to hit away successfully or she cuts over the block when you block angle. One idea is to use the doubling up technique on her favorite area (crosscourt) and to let her hit line without a block or a defender. A way to make it riskier for her to hit line (if she figures out your are blocking crosscourt and digging crosscourt) is to serve her wide, thus making the line shot appear even thinner and less attractive to try. With a set closer to the sideline it will encourage her to continue to hit angle where you and your partner are doubling up. Block and dig angle over and over again. Don't let the player off the hook by switching it up to dig line until your team has exhausted the success of digging her crosscourt hits and shots. Take away her favorite hit and make her hit only what she does not prefer to do.

This particular chapter contains some of the best information I have gathered over the thirty years I've been playing and coaching beach volleyball. It's exciting to think about defense and fun to have available so many interesting ways to dig your opponent. Early in a player's career, getting the basics of defense are important, but it is also important to think outside of the box. Use your brain and get into the possibilities available to you every time you step onto the court. Your observation skills are important because if the opponent has not evolved enough to look at your team as their hitters are hitting, then some of the gamesmanship of these tactics will be less effective. If your opponent is struggling just to return your serve or just to hit it into the court, then, of course, simplicity is the best option. However, by virtue of you reading this book you are curious enough to know there is so much more strategy that can be implemented on defense than just your standard "read and run" defense.

The variety of defensive options I've discussed such as the juke, baiting the hitter, and the creep are all legitimate defensive techniques, but you have to know yourself and know if you have the ability to execute them. I coached a player who was particularly quick to move forward on defense but was slow to turn and run to chase balls. What she did was make sure her starting spot on defense was deep in the court so it was almost impossible to hit a ball over her head, and anything in front of her she was able to touch. She knew her strengths and used them to the best of her ability. Much of what was discussed requires planning, a good memory, and courage. There are not many matches won by players who do not possess the ability to learn from their mistakes and to take some calculated risks. Defense is the chess game of beach volleyball and to be a good defender requires dedication, patience, and most importantly, the spirit of the defender. My definition of a great defender is the willingness to go after every shot and attempt to touch every hit. Make it the team policy because as in most sports, defense wins games.

Angie Akers and Holly McPeak

©Brian White

10 STRATEGIC OPTIONS

There is your basic offense and then there is all the really fun stuff. The stuff that irritates your opponent and creates momentum, but most importantly adds dimension to your offense. Hitting on two, setting over on two, having a fitness level that allows for dig after dig after dig, are all excellent strategic advantages.

When I began playing on the beach in 1987, I played in a tournament at Pismo Beach, California, against Kathy Gregory. I was playing with Liz and at that time we were both on the national team and as fit and strong as we've probably ever been in our entire lives. Liz and I could both touch over ten feet and were very powerful hitters. What I didn't know at that time, but certainly learned later, were the nuances of beach volleyball. Kathy verbally tormented Liz and me (something she was famous for), as she shot the ball over on one, on two or she simply outsmarted us. We were younger and fitter coming from the US National Team and she schooled us. Although Kathy was twenty-plus years our senior, she made us look like amateurs (which we were at that point). Having the fitness without the experience and skill wasn't enough for us at that point—especially me.

When is a great time to use an over-on-one attack? I have found as a player and coach that when a defender gets an early read on a poorly placed cut shot (a wide, easy, slow shot) that instead of making the dig, tomahawk the ball back over. This over-on-one should be to the opponents' deep corners—which are usually wide open at this moment because they just attacked from the net. Former professional player and 1996 Olympian Linda Hanley describes this as the "hero or zero" play. The defender can look like the biggest hero for making the quick read and attacking the attack shot with a single contact, or look like the biggest zero for giving the opponent a poorly-placed ball, or worse yet, making an error. Many of these types of plays happen on hard-hit rebound digs that are accidentally hit back to the opponents' side, which is why they score. On the other hand a deliberate one-over contact that is timed well can be a huge momentum changer. The over-on-one attack should be used when the opportunity is available, not as a play bred from impatience or fatigue. An ideal time for an over-on-one is late in a long rally as the defenders tire of running down shots and when they lack the motivation or conditioning to run down a well-placed, on-one attack.

Playing the ball into the net

Occasionally a sharp cut shot can be dug, but not dug back off the net. Instead of trying to pull the dig back into the court, hit the ball into the net. This deliberate hit with the ball into the net can potentially create a better dig for the setter to set. Announcing "net" will alert the defender's partner that she will need to set the ball from the rebound off the net. This play takes guts as it's against most players' instincts to deliberately hit a ball into the net. If there is no alternative, it makes perfect sense. The beach volleyball net typically has some slack that allows the ball to get hung up for a moment in the bottom rope/cable; therefore, it provides a type of momentary cradle for the ball. This cradle effect allows the setter an extra moment to get low and play the ball out of the net and give her partner a set.

Hitting on two

Attacking on two was brought to the women's game by 1996 Olympic Gold Medalist Jackie Silva from Brazil. Jackie played on the WPVA (Women's Professional Volleyball Association) and was the tour's MVP and top money earner for several years in the 1980s. Jackie was a former Brazilian indoor national team setter. She had excellent vision of the court and her favorite on-two attack was a back set over the net to the shallow front area of the court of the opponent's side. Because Jackie always hand set on the beach, it was difficult to anticipate her attacking on two; therefore, she was highly successful. Very few players back set over the net as an on-two attack, but it can be a very effective way to force opponents to make adjustments in their defensive base position. I was very lucky to play with Jackie and together we won the US Open at Venice Beach after losing the first round of the tournament. Jackie was so upset about our loss that we argued that evening for hours about what we could have changed and done better and who was to blame for the loss. I don't think either of us slept much but we came back the next day and went through the losers bracket and won the event. Not only was Jackie a great setter, but she was a very competitive woman who hated to lose.

Another effective time to attack on two is when the blocker is serving and running up. The setter on the receiving team must be alert to this opportunity. It's much more effective to hit on two at this time because the blocker is not typically prepared to defend while sprinting to the net. Most primary blockers will elect to serve line-to-line because this allows them the shortest distance to net. This means that the setter is hitting to the angle from their side to the opponents' court. This crosscourt swing is typically easiest for a right-handed player from the left side of the court or a left-handed player from the right. It is most common for the smaller player to play the right. This player is typically the person who gets served more balls, and therefore, the taller player can participate more in the offense with the on-two attack.

Hitting on two is a good way to accomplish two things. One, ease the pressure on the player being served and, two, potentially make the opponent choose to serve the player who is hitting on two to stop her from scoring. In 1995, while on the AVP Tour, I played in Madison Square Garden. At that time, it was just a four-team event consisting of a semifinal and a final. I was playing with

Liz, who was only a few months post-op from a broken kneecap and ACL repair. Liz, of course, was served every ball to test her health and stamina. I think I must have hit or dumped on two nearly fifty percent of the balls that Liz passed. We placed second in that event because we had used our strengths to win. Liz had extraordinary ball control and I could hit on two or set over to create offensive opportunities for us.

Another option is to run a back set. When the blocker follows the hitter who is hitting a back set, an opportunity for an on-two attack has opened up. The setter now has no blocker in front of her plus an open net. A simple forward set over the net short can easily score if the defender does not adjust out of base defensive position. If the setter does not hand set, she can attack on two with an easy roll shot forward instead of setting the back set. What the attacker (setter) has to be aware of is when the blocker does not follow the hitter on the back set, but instead drops off the net to play defense. Hitting on two is much less effective against a two-down defense but if the blocker pulls, the setter can set the back set on and the hitter can hit without a block, which is still a good outcome.

In transition, why set when you can hit? Transition is one of the best times to attack on two. The opponent's defense is typically not as stationary or set as it is during the offense's first attempt to side out. As the rally progresses, the blocker and defender may not be as alert to defend on-two attack. The risk is that hitting on two is hard to execute when the setter (hitter) is off-balance. If the primary blocker, who also is not receiving the majority of the serves, has an opportunity to end the rally with an on-two swing, she should capitalize on a chance for a kill. Hitting on two can ease the pressure on the defender to score from every dig and provide a much-needed swing for the blocker.

Nancy Reno played with Holly McPeak for several years in the 1990s; they won numerous events and were World Champions. Nancy hit a large percentage of passes from Holly on two and this worked extremely well for the team. However, constant off-balance attacking ended up injuring Nancy's shoulder and by the 1996 Olympics she was hitting at sixty percent of her original strength. The unfortunate thing was that the team's success was built on Holly's extraordinary ball control and defensive skills coupled with Nancy's excellent blocking and on-two attack. When the team no longer had Nancy's on-two, they had to rely on Holly's ability to side out and Nancy's side out swing had diminished from its original strength. This, unfortunately, changed their chemistry and they finished fifth at the 1996 Olympics. Holly continued to play and chose other big blockers which she developed into on-two hitters and played in two more Olympics with two different partners.

Standing and hitting on two can also be done effectively if you are a hand setter. As I mentioned earlier, during our tournament in New York I played with Liz after one of her many knee surgeries in the 1996 Olympic Trials. I used the over on two routinely but with a different twist. I always set with my hands and our coach, Dede Bodnar, a former indoor setter at Cal Poly (California Polytechnic State University San Luis Obispo), taught me to hit on two from a standing position. I would pretend to prepare to hand set, but instead I would use my right hand to hit a back cut shot over the net (Liz played the right). My standing right handed dump shot to their right front was rarely dug. For us to do this effectively, we needed the pass to be high enough for me to set and close enough to the net so I could be in a good position to hit on two. Although Liz's knee was extremely stiff and swollen, her ball control when passing was, as always, very good. Liz was served just about every ball and with my hitting on two, we limited her jumps and forced our opponents to test me on serve receive. Liz and I did not qualify for the Olympics, but at that time we had finished in the top three in several events with our style of play. It just wasn't enough on that particular day.

Hitting on two with a spike, back bump over, overhead standing hit, or setting back are all good ways to add to your offense. However, overdoing it can put the hitter out of sync and create unforced errors. Selective use is better than overuse. Frankly, once a team hits a ball on two, the opponent is forever on high alert for the on two and typically more prepared the second time and subsequent times to defend the attack. Mix it up.

Throughout this book, I've discussed many different options for defensive and offensive strategies but hitting on two or over on one is simply one of the most rewarding and satisfying things you can do to an opponent. It takes the wind out of any team's sails and it always earns a big smile from your teammate—both worth becoming a hero over.

The psychological edge

Players who seem to reach new heights in their game usually are committed to conditioning. A perfect example is Brooke Niles, former AVP professional and current beach volleyball head coach at Florida State. She is only five feet eight inches tall but with her dedication to conditioning, Brook has transformed her body and her game. Brooke has invested in a conditioning program that is tailored to her needs and will build her strength and speed. She is one of the quickest players who can run down just about any ball, who looks, and can hit any area of the court that is open. Brooke has also overcome serious knee and shoulder injuries mostly due to her commitment to strength and conditioning. Her conditioning gives Brooke a mental edge. When she walks onto the court, she knows she has left no stone unturned and has done everything possible within her power to be the best player she can be. There is peace in having that knowledge—the knowledge that you've done everything to prepare and now you just have to play.

My edge was always my jump serve and my ability to hit an extremely hard ball. I was blessed with a great jump serve and I had a powerful arm. I always made sure in the warm-up that my opponent was reminded of it as well. I know it was a huge strength of mine and my psychological edge.

Some players like to play the "don't talk to the opponent" game or the "let's pretend we are friends" game prior to the match or even during the match, but it's all part of the bigger picture. People are always looking for weaknesses in their opponent and always looking for an edge in a match. It might be a small thing—something you're not even aware that's happening. But don't let your guard down—not even just a bit. That competitive edge may matter during the course of a match. I remember playing against Janice Opalinski Harrer in the early days of the WPVA and she used a stalling tactic of slowly wiping the sand off her body. Sometimes she hadn't even hit the ground! Janice would use this tactic especially when she needed to change the momentum of the match. She would walk over to the sideline, grab a towel, and slowly wipe the sand off herself. This practice was a great stalling tactic (until the rules changed and it wasn't allowed) and irritated the crap out of me personally. It worked somewhat as it was a great way to get under the skin of your opponent and for many years it was perfectly acceptable and almost expected from players.

It's a great game

I was fortunate to play beach volleyball for many years and that is my main motivation for writing this book. Just about every sunny day I wish that I were still able to go out there and enjoy playing again. I am so thrilled that it is an official NCAA sport for women and that the USA has produced so many top players, both men and women. One of my best friends, Liz, who I talk about often in this book, asked me why I wanted to write a book. I've really thought about that and what I wanted to do was get all these thoughts out on paper for future generations of coaches and players. We also talked about how when we played you just didn't share your knowledge with anyone because partners came and went. We had a very long tour schedule, sometimes up to sixteen events plus international tournaments, and partner switching was extremely common. We carefully guarded what we knew about ourselves, our opponents, and any weaknesses we had. Currently, the NCAA programs and numerous professional options have created some great knowledge-sharing opportunities. As I mentioned earlier, much of what I learned about strategy was when I became a coach and those players I trained trusted me enough to share their strategies with me. For that, I am forever grateful and really wish I could have known as much when I was still playing.

I know there are many different opinions on how to play this game I love so much. I just had to get this information out of my head and available to those who seek multiple perspectives so others could enjoy the great sport of beach volleyball even more.

GLOSSARY OF TERMS

A LOOKER – a player who takes a look at the defense during her approach to hit.

ANGLE – just as it is in the indoor game, this is a hard-driven spike hit to the angle.

BAIT BLOCKING – showing that you are taking a particular area of the court but instead, at the last moment, jumping into the opposite area during the block.

BLOCKING BALL – the most aggressive block taking everything that you see and reading the hitter.

CAMPING OUT – when someone sits in a specific area of the court time and time again for so long she can have a campfire.

CHICKEN WING – reaction to a hard-driven spike that is coming at your shoulder one arm is bent like a chicken wing in order to block the ball and make a legal dig.

CUT SHOT – an extreme angle hit that is off-speed and lands usually within a few feet from the sideline and as close to the net as possible.

GATER – a mid-body dig that is open-handed and your hands are shaped like an alligator's mouth, only used on hard-driven hits.

"I" DEFENSE – usually used when someone is hitting out of the middle, lining up directly behind the blocker in order not to telegraph what half of the court you and your partner are defending.

JUKE – fake one way when you intend to move to the opposite direction.

JUMBO SHRIMP – a long, deep crosscourt lob shot that has a big arch on it like a shrimp which goes over the head of the defender.

LINE SHOT – either a lob shot over the blocker's hands that should reach the end line or a shot that is over a retreating blocker's head, also as close to the end line as possible.

LISTENING TO THE CALL – when the defender reacts to what the opponent's setter is calling for the shot.

ONE-OFF – a serve to the player who has not been served to all match long, typically at the end of the match.

POKE – a closed-hand contact at the ball, usually as an offensive play but can also be used as a defensive contact on an overhead dig.

PULLING – when the blocker decides to not block based on an offset or as a defensive strategy to defend a particular hitter.

RELEASING – what the setting partner does when her partner is served to set the ball.

ROLODEX – the history of shots, hits that the opponent is making, and the order in which they hit them.

RUNNING DOWN – when a defender runs down a shot.

SIDE OUT – breaking the opponent's serve but now it's called point scoring.

SHOT MODE – when a player is in a groove of hitting off speed shots and will not swing at a ball.

TOMAHAWK – an overhead dig, with hands together, for a ball that is shot, not hard-driven.

WATERFALL – a short roll shot over the block or short in front of the defender.

Angela Rock

©John Bartelt

About the Author

ANGELA ROCK is one of America's most celebrated and decorated volleyball players. She is an Olympian both as a player and as a coach—Team USA's most valuable player in 1985 and a member of the San Diego State University (SDSU) Hall of Fame and the Beach Volleyball Hall of Fame. Rock coached the US beach volleyball team at the 1996 Olympics in Atlanta, the inaugural year of the sport in the Olympic Games.

Rock earned her bachelor's in psychology from SDSU, a master's in physical education from Azusa Pacific University, and a master's in education from National University. In addition, she is a former San Diego firefighter and a mentor to future Olympians.

While at San Diego State University, Rock participated on two NCAA Final Four volleyball teams in 1981 and 1982 and received First Team All American honors as an outside hitter on the Aztecs' women's NCAA volleyball team in 1984.

Internationally, Rock played on the US national team for five years, and participated in the 1986 Goodwill Games, the 1986 World Championships, the 1987 Pan American Games, and most notably, the 1988 Olympic Games in Seoul, South Korea, where the Americans placed seventh.

From 1987 to 2000, Rock was a major force on both the Women's Professional Volleyball Association and the Fédération Internationale de Volleyball tours. She won 27 events, including 12 titles in 1991 when she was voted the tour's best hitter.

Rock also served as assistant coach at the University of California Santa Barbara and as head coach at the University of Alaska Fairbanks, a Division II university, where she set a school record for Pacific West Conference victories. In addition, Rock coached club volleyball at Rancho Santa Fe, Surf, and Coast, all premier clubs in her hometown of San Diego. She was also the head coach at Southwestern College in Chula Vista, California.

When not playing golf or enjoying her garden, Rock is currently a professor of health and exercise science at Southwestern College. She hopes to retire to Bend, Oregon, where she can golf, fish, hike, and enjoy wintertime activities.

Made in the USA
Las Vegas, NV
12 August 2021